chicago's
50 best
places to
take
children

By Clare La Plante

universe publishing

First published in the United States of America in 2003
by UNIVERSE PUBLISHING
A Division of Rizzoli International Publications, Inc.
300 Park Avenue South
New York, NY 10010
www.rizzoliusa.com

© Clare La Plante 2004
Cover design by Paul Kepple and Jude Buffum @ Headcase Design
www.headcasedesign.com
Cover illustration by Mary Lynn Blasutta
Interior design by Headcase Design

2004 2005 2006 2007/ 10 9 8 7 6 5 4 3 2 1

Distributed in the U.S. trade by St. Martin's Press, New York

Printed in the United States of America

ISBN: 0-7893-1078-3

Library of Congress Catalog Control Number: 2004108833

contents

To my parents

Acknowledgments

I want to thank those who ventured to the Best Places with me, and those who offered their wisdom of the city. They include Henry and Will Klauke, James Hanafee, Chris Preissing and Mary Kane, Andy Kostrub, Fran, Willy, Chris and Lizzy Caan, Caroline and Erik Beckwith, Paul Simpson, Joe Clary, Joe Hanafee, Elizabeth La Plante, Michael Allaway, Lynn La Plante, Catherine La Plante, and Mary Ruth Clarke. Also, thanks to the great people at Universe Publishing: Kathleen Jayes for entrusting this project to me, and my editor Holly Rothman, for her patience and unerring editorial eye. As always, many thanks to my wonderful agent Arielle Eckstut for bringing this project my way.

introduction

Getting around Chicago with a kids-eye view was a learning experience. What I learned is that we're a great arts town— and not just for grownups. We have some of the most innovative, accessible theater for kids anywhere, including DePaul's Chicago Playworks for Families and Young Audiences, the Piven Theatre, and the Puppet Parlor. We have amazing art centers, such as the Lillstreet Art Center, where you can take awesome art classes. We also have nature in spades, from the Morton Arboretum out in the west suburbs to the lovely Chicago Botanic Gardens to the north to the sublime Osaka Gardens in Hyde Park.

After visiting well-known places and hidden treasures, I thought to myself: It's no wonder that so many Chicago kids grow up to be really interesting adults—Chicago and otherwise—leaders in the arts, science, and humanities. When you have access to the above mentioned spots, plus kids humanities and film festivals, along with some of the best museums in the world, you can't help but develop an interesting side.

And the beauty of it? Most of the best Chicago kid stuff is affordable and accessible. You can get to nearly all these places by public transportation (except for some of the far suburb locales), and admission to most is less than $10. Also, for all our big-town benefits, we're a small town at heart. At nearly every one of the 50 featured places, you can get individualized attention. (They'll give you customized talks, tours, meals, songs, etc.)

For each of my visits, I tried to bring along a Chicago kid—or at least interview one or two at the scene. (Many thanks to my nephews Henry, Will, and James for being willing accomplices.) These kids helped me to see what was really special (and not so much, in some cases) about a place, and also shared their favorite activities at each.

What I found is that Chicago kids like Chicago originals: The parks that have stood for decades and still welcome kids to their boundaries, the quirky restaurants that have seen generations of Chicagoans come and go or the museums that offer just the right Chicago touch: a miniature Chicago grocery store or a history of the city.

I tried to include these "must do's" in each entry, along with tips on making the most of your visit. I've also included ideal ages, but these are merely guidelines—obviously adults who love and know the kids in their lives will be the best judges.

What I found, however, is that the most important ingredient for teaching your kids how to enjoy Chicago is for you to enjoy it—and them—yourself. For these 50 Best Places and other Chicago jewels, simply relish the time you have with the child in your life, whether it be your child, grandchild, friend, niece, nephew, cousin, little sister or brother. When all is said and done, that's the most important thing. Chicago just provides the settings.

chicago's
50 best

(A to Z)

the adler planetarium

✳ *1300 S. Lake Shore Drive, Chicago, IL 60605*
312-922-STAR
Ideal Age Group: 4 to 17
Admission: Adults $13; seniors $12; children $11
www.adlerplanetarium.org

star gazing and other night sky treats

For those who like a cosmic view of the world, check out the Adler Planetarium, another jewel in the crown of the Museum Campus, a conglomeration of three museums on the banks of Lake Michigan just east of the Loop, which also includes the Field Museum and the Shedd Aquarium. The Adler Planetarium is a star-gazing treat that's taught generations of Chicagoans how to look at the sky. This building is 35,000 square feet of exhibits, including two full-size planetarium theaters, interactive exhibits, ancient astronomy instruments, and scale models of the solar system.

Most visitors take advantage of the theaters. First, there's the Sky Theater, the traditional, in-the-round planetarium that projects a re-creation of the night's starry sky onto a 68-foot dome. The first planetarium in the Western hemisphere, this laid-back (literally, the seats go way back) opportunity to star gaze has been around since 1930. It's awesome, and a little overwhelming to those just beginning to understand the puniness of our home planet. You may be well advised to read up on the solar system before going. (It will make identifying different constellations more fun, too!)

The second theater, the StarRider, is perfect for those who grew up with computer games and all things high-tech. This interactive, digital gallery has operating controls in the armrests to help you blast off into the stratosphere.

The museum also contains many exhibition galleries, including Bringing Heavens to Earth, where you can learn—in a hands-on manner—how the cultures of the world, including the Egyptian pharaohs and Assyrian kings, incorporated astronomy into their lives, and what a powerful hold astronomy has had over humans since the beginning of time.

Another fun gallery for kids is Stranded in an Alien Lab, where they can become a space explorer billions of miles from home. Designed for ages 8 to 11, this exhibit gives a hands-on experience of other worlds.

If you have a real astronomy buff in your household, you probably shouldn't miss Far Out Friday, the first Friday of each month, when the museum is open from 5 to 10 p.m. (admission is $15 for adults and $12 for kids and seniors). Kids can bring their old or new telescopes for instruction and tips on use. You can also hear lectures by famous space scientists and get your stargazing questions answered. (Note: The Far Out Friday programmers are very topical: They're already covering trips to Mars.)

Of course, there may be one more good reason to check out Far Out Friday: Most die-hard Chicagoans say that the Adler Planetarium offers one of the most beautiful views of the city. Nothing beats gazing onto the skyline on a summer night, especially after viewing the cosmos.

american girl place

* *111 E. Chicago Avenue, Chicago, IL 60611*
800-AG-PLACE
Ideal Age Group: 5 to 10
Admission: Free (costs come later!)
www.americangirl.com

dolls, dolls, dolls!

If there is a girl under 12 in your life, chances are that you'll
be cajoled into an American Girl Place pilgrimage. Not for the
faint of heart, this three-story, 37,500-square-foot doll haven
on Chicago Avenue, just west of Michigan Avenue near the
Magnificent Mile, can keep you entrapped for hours, and
tempt you into spending way too much money.

What draws the crowds to this place? Chicago's American Girl Place was the first American Girl Store ever. (Now
New York has one on Fifth Avenue.) That means it was
Ground Zero for Molly, Samantha, Addie, and other dolls that
were the brainchild of a Middleton, Wisconsin, teacher who
created eight original oversized dolls that came with six-chap-
ter books detailing their history and lives. Girls come from all
over the country to visit this holy ground.

And they want to buy stuff, a lot of it. For example, dolls
run about $90; furniture can run as high as several hundred.
Add to that clothes, furniture, and accessories, and you get
the idea.

It all feels so painless. As you enter the ground floor, the
perennially cheery staff—with absolutely no sign of fatigue—
will greet you, and point you in the right direction, whether it's
the doll beauty salon, or the American Girl Theater, with live
musical performances on the basement level, or the top floor
and American Girl Café, where the girls can dine with their

dolls—the dolls are seated in high chairs that attach to the tables. (One bright spot for adults is the amazing view across Michigan Avenue of the original Water Tower.)

If you know you're going to visit the store, your best bet is to get there early on a weekday. If you get there right at 10 a.m., when the store opens, you can even find metered parking a little west on Chicago Avenue. (Make sure you call ahead for lunch or tea reservations.)

Also, keep a firm hand on your budget. There are ways to enjoy the store without spending a bundle. For example, one friend brought her young daughter and friends to the cafe for her daughter's birthday party, and had the girls bring their own beloved rag dolls for tea. (It's allowed!) Or give your daughter her own budget before entering the store—which would fit right in with the thrifty and resourceful qualities the books and dolls are always promoting.

However, for adults, the real fun may be when you're done. You can stroll up Michigan Avenue and take in all the amazing sights—the megastores, the people rushing by, and the small boutiques. Or you can cross the street and walk through Water Tower Place—an eight-level shopping mall extravaganza, with everything from Marshall Fields to Lord & Taylor to Foodlife, an upscale food court. (And for celebrity watchers, Oprah Winfrey lives in the attached condominiums.)

The John Hancock Center is also across the street, which, for a while, was the tallest building in the world. For those who can stand the heights, take a trip up to the observatory at the top and look out over 80 miles and four states. That might help ease the pain of several hundred dollars of doll clothing in your shopping bag.

american science & surplus

❋ *5316 N. Milwaukee Avenue, Chicago, IL 60630*
773-763-0313
Ideal Age Group: 4 and older
Admission: Free
www.sciplus.com

In the market for fake eyeballs? Trick pens? Army knives? This cool gadget store has it.

A bizarrely diverse store that sells army backpacks next to (fake) squishy eyeballs, this is the store Bart Simpson would patronize if he lived in Chicago. Since 1937, American Science & Surplus has run a very successful catalog company—and is a mecca of sorts for science geeks everywhere. The home office is right at a Milwaukee Avenue strip mall in the heart of Chicago's Little Warsaw.

The store was founded by a Chicagoan named Al Luebbers who had an interest in optics and collected discarded lenses. (Who knew you could make money in discarded lenses?) He eventually expanded his business to include other doo-dads and eventually passed the business along to his son, who, in turn, sold it. Now it's in the hands of Phillip Crane—not the Illinois State Rep, but rather a self-professed science geek. So it's in good hands.

It's a kids' wonderland. Of course, adults can come out big winners here, too, since kids can find bona fide treasures here for well under five bucks—stuff like invisible ink, bony finger pens, and butterfly yoyos. For serious science buffs, you can find first-rate telescopes, microscopes, and science books. For kids who like to build things, check out the tools, home gadgets, and other fix-it necessities.

Studious types will find notebooks, office supplies, and organizers. It's a smorgasbord!

The quirky stuff, of course, is the most fun: a skull desk fountain that flows with "blood," a brain jello mold, and a robot claw. You'll also find things like Ecumenical Boxers, which include a fighting nun. They call it a "unique mixture of industrial, military, and educational items, with an emphasis on science and education." You'll call it fun. And they encourage browsing. The clerks are great—helpful and patient.

Make sure you pick up a catalog while you're there, too, and enjoy the catalog descriptions. The blurb for a magnifying mirror reads: "This is one scary mirror for a bad complexion day, but if you really want to see every detail, this is the one you want."

Kids'll also get a kick out of the amazing variety of "surplus," including soil test kits, a carry-around rainbow, and a plain old box of rocks.

Once you've finished browsing, don't leave Milwaukee Avenue without trying some homemade pierogis at nearby restaurants. Visit the Pierogi Inn at 4801 N. Milwaukee, or the Red Apple at 3121 N. Milwaukee, whose all-you-can-eat buffet will keep you couch-bound for days. Atkins dieters should stay home.

the ARTiFACT center/
the spertus museum

※ *618 S. Michigan Avenue, Chicago IL 60605*
312-322-1747
Ideal Age Group: 8 to 13 (although they also have
preschool activities)
Admission: Adults $5; children and seniors $3; Fridays free
www.spertus.edu

an archaeology dig for fun

Nearly hidden in the South Loop, right next to Columbia
College and across the street from Grant Park, stands an
unassuming museum with a wonderful basement treat for
kids. The Spertus Museum of Judaica—which holds art and
artifacts about the Jewish culture and religion—also houses
the ARTiFACT Center, which since 1989 has been teaching
kids the beauty of the dig, to the tune of more than 10,000
kids a year. The museum reserves mornings for school and
community groups. Afternoons from 1 to 4:30 p.m. (1-3 on
Fridays) are open to the public.

In this space kids from ages 8 to 13 will participate in
excavating a tel—or mound of earth—where layers of civiliza-
tion have been buried. All of the activities aim, says Susan
Marcus, the curator of ARTiFACT Center, to "teach children to
consider what they have in common with those in the past,
and to put a face on ancient history."

For the cost of museum admission (which is only $3 for
children and $5 for adults), kids can find replicas of ancient
treasures, and then bring them to the Pottery Laboratory to
find out who lived when and where. (And parents, don't worry,
the "dirt" of the tel is really hypoallergenic sand.)

Museum employees lead the digs, and these educators teach the diggers how to excavate methodically, keeping track of all their finds, just like professional archaeologists would.

The ARTiFACT Center also contains six learning centers. In addition to the Pottery Laboratory, these include sites on ancient alphabets, music, and traded goods. All are interactive. (Kids can write ancient languages, play ancient instruments, and play math games that teach them about weights and measures.)

Although younger kids are welcomed, the museum discourages those under 5 from taking place in the dig. Instead, preschoolers can have fun at the Israelite House, where they can play in a 3000-year-old home—donning clothing, cooking in a little kitchen, and playing with animals and in sand.

The Center also hosts special programs throughout the year, such as puppetry and storytelling, arts and crafts and community arts projects, including a recent one where the kids "painted out pollution." They repainted dark images on a 3-D work with more positive images.

While you're there, you may want to take advantage of the whole museum—it contains a host of art and historical figures. Check out the Chicago Jewish Archives, a treasure chest of letters, journals, and photos from Chicago Jewish immigrants and citizens. A caution for parents, however: The museum contains a rather graphic Holocaust Exhibit, which they recommend only for those 12 and older.

the art institute of chicago

✳ *111 S. Michigan Avenue, Chicago, IL 60603*
312-443-3600
Ideal Age Group: 6 and up
Admission (suggested donations): Adults $10; children
and seniors $6; children under 5, free
www.artic.edu

high culture on michigan avenue

If you want to introduce your kids to some pretty amazing
stuff, head down Michigan Avenue to our version of the
Louvre. The Art Institute of Chicago offers world-class art—
everything from paintings from the Middle Ages to today;
Ancient Greek, Roman, and Egyptian art; and one of the
largest Monet collections outside of France.

The formal galleries and hushed tones might seem
unkid-like, but with the right attitude, your kids will fit right in.
If you need some official advice, start with Behind the Lions:
A Family Guide to the Art Institute of Chicago, or Looking at
Art Together: A Parent Guide to the Art Institute of Chicago,
both available in their first-floor museum store. Or, of course,
you could wing it yourself. Here are some tips.

One parent I know brings her kids to the museum shop
before they enter the galleries themselves, and each child
picks out several postcards of works from the museum. They
then go on a scavenger hunt looking for their postcard art.
Another fun way to view the art is to bring a sketch pad and
let the kids draw their favorite painting or sculpture. Very
young kids are often happy just looking at a few favorite
paintings again and again.

If you have kids who like to touch (a definite no-no in the Art Institute environs), you can visit the Touch Gallery, which, as its name suggests, allows a tactile experience. (The participating sculptures are treated with a special protective coating.) Or remove temptation altogether and visit the Thorne Rooms, really cool miniature models of living spaces from different places and times behind panes of glass.

The Kraft Education Center on the lower level also offers family programs—and registration is not usually required (admission is included in the fee for entry to the museum). These workshops, for which kids must be accompanied by an adult, include programs such as Sky-O-Ramas, where kids make their own diorama of the winter sky, or Crazy Carpets, where young ones make textile art inspired by Picasso, or Drawing in the Galleries, which teaches rudimentary drawing skills with the help of masterpieces. The Center also offers story time, one Sunday per month, with each chosen story related to one of the art exhibits.

If you get hungry, you can grab a snack at one of the museum's several restaurant/cafes, or you can stroll up Adams Street to the Berghoff—one of Chicago's oldest and most venerable restaurants. It's more than 100 years old, and offers homemade German food and Chicago memorabilia—don't miss their fresh rye bread and root beer for kids. Or you may even consider hopping on one of the double-decker tour buses that stop right outside the Institute, and visit various Loop sites. (Call 773-648-5000 or visit www.chicagodoubledecker.com for more information.)

One final note: Before you leave the museum, don't forget to take a picture with the famous lions that guard the entrance. These are the same lions that don Bears helmets and Cubs hats on those rare occasions when a Chicago team is winning.

brookfield zoo

3300 Golf Road, Brookfield, IL 60513

708-485-0263

Ideal Age Group: Stroller to teens

Admission: Adults $8; children $4; seniors $4; children 2 and under, free. Parking, $8 a car (free days scheduled during fall and winter)

www.brookfieldzoo.com

the chicago zoo

This 216-acre zoo is one of the largest, and best, in the country. Located in suburban Brookfield—around 14 miles west of the Loop—this animal wonderland offers an escape, as well as an education in many of the world's creatures. Since it's a bit of a distance from downtown, make it a day trip. Make sure you bring snacks, strollers, and plenty of energy.

It's not hard to get to. If you decide to drive, it's pretty much a straight shot down the Eisenhower, or you can take Metra's Burlington Northern line and exit at the Zoo stop. Open year-round, it's the perfect antidote to cabin (or city) fever any time of the year. April and May bring the school crowds, but fall and winter are when crowds are sparse, and the animals curious and calm (they also offer free days in the winter). Of course, spring and summer offer the full beauty of the flowers and fountains. If you must come with the crowds, come early in the morning or later in the afternoon.

Any time you make it here, you'll be glad you did. Brookfield Zoo has scads of major exhibits, including Tropic World, a microcosm of many of the rain forests around the world, including those of South America, Asia, and Africa. It includes a 20-foot waterfall, vultures, gibbons, and orangutans (including two new zoo babies—a baby Western

Lowland Gorilla and a baby orangutan).

Other favorite exhibits include the Seven Seas Dolphin Show, where you can see dolphins dance and play with their trainers—and they listen, too! Also, the Salt Creek Wilderness offers a quarter-mile trail around a small lake that gives its travelers a look into the workings of the Illinois ecosystems—there's even a dragonfly marsh at the north end.

The two-acre Hammill Family Play Zoo allows kids hands-on learning experiences, including building habitats, painting murals, and planting gardens. In the Zoo Within A Zoo, kids can dress up like veterinarians and "treat" animals or pretend to be zookeepers or other zoo workers.

Don't miss Brookfield Zoo's annual Holiday Magic Festival, where the zoo decorates the trees with nearly half a million Christmas lights. The zookeepers let the animals stay up later than usual so patrons can carol to them. During or after the festivities, you can warm up with hot apple cider. Other special events are scheduled throughout the year—you can attend breakfast with Santa or celebrate Groundhog or Arbor Day with the zoo.

Perhaps the best thing of all about the Brookfield Zoo is that you can always just pop in—even in the dead of winter—and know that your day will be filled with beauty and nature. Perfect for strollers, kids, and adults who like to walk outside and visit with animals.

the chicago
botanic garden

✳ *1000 Lake Cook Road, Glencoe, IL 60022*

847-835-5440

Ideal Age Group: Stroller and up

Admission: Free (parking: $8.75 per car; $5.75 seniors)

flowers, lagoons, bridges, and special treats

Although really in Glencoe, a suburb 25 miles north of down-town Chicago, the Chicago Botanic Garden proudly takes the name of the city and is a refuge for nature lovers from all over. It's conveniently located right off the Edens Expressway, and it's right on the north branch of the Chicago River bike trail, which starts at Devon and Caldwell Avenues (bikers and walk-ers get in free!). You can continue to bike throughout the garden, or you can walk. However you go, you'll find colorful flowers and plants, special outdoor exhibits, and kid-friendly grounds. (Although you can't pick the flowers!)

If going to a garden sounds as exciting to your kids as a trip to the dentist, you might want to explain before you go that this is so much more than a garden. In fact, it's 26 gar-dens all in one, with 1.9 million plants spread out over 385 acres and eight lagoons.

Some of these gardens include the magical three-island Japanese Garden, with bridges, sculpted trees, and a recre-ated 17th-century Samurai retreat. Or Spider Island, with native trees, grasses, and wild flowers that lead to a sanctuary by one of the lagoons, or the Aquatic Garden, where you walk over a boardwalk garden of water lilies and lotuses.

There's never a bad time to visit the Botanic Garden (it's

open year-round except for Christmas Day). In fact, you may want to come in winter, when kids can roam the inside gardens, including the educational greenhouses, with rainforest plants, exotic cacti from the desert, and a tactile garden exhibit, where kids can touch and smell really cool plants (like the one that curls up when you touch it).

In the summer, you may want to check out the Fruit and Vegetable Garden, where you can see demonstrations and exhibits of goodies such as herbs, peppers, and grapes. Call ahead of time and find out if they are featuring one of their special exhibits, like the Railway Garden, with a model train running through 12 simulated national park settings. These may cost a few dollars above admission price.

You might want to arm kids with a sketchpad beforehand to capture their favorite plant, flower—or insect! Or let them choose some seeds from the Garden store so you can start your own garden together, back at home. It's also a great place to picnic on a spring or summer day—just make sure you eat within designated areas.

The main building has a great café, for both kids and adults—with inexpensive, easy-to-eat food, some of it even healthy!—and you can eat inside or out, weather permitting.

For kids interested in the Earth, the Botanic Garden offers a slew of wonderful programming for children and families, many held in the Children's Garden. You can sign up for summer camp (but do so early—classes fill fast!).

chic-a-go-go!

❀ *For more information, write*
  1507 E. 53rd Street, #617, Chicago, IL 60615
  Admission: Free
  www.roctober.com
  info@roctober.com

an indie-music american bandstand

Described as "Mr. Rogers goes to Studio 54," this dance party cable access show works for the young hipster in your life. Produced by indie music lover Jake Austin, and directed by his wife, University of Chicago professor Jacqueline Stewart, this Channel 19 dance extravaganza has been charming Chicago audiences since 1996. To participate, all you need to do is show up at the cable station—no tickets necessary—and dance. (Costumes optional.)

A young actor, Miss Mia, and a rat puppet named Ratso host the event, telling corny jokes and generally overseeing the chaos. Austin says his show is the "Barney" antidote—the music is original, edgy, and diverse. They've hosted everyone from Poi Dog Pondering to Blues Legend Andre Williams who, like all the musical guests, lip sync to their albums as the crowd dances around, doing *Chic-A-Go-Go!* favorites like the "El Train Line."

The show caters to kids and it's appropriate for all ages. They won't play any songs with offensive lyrics, and at any given time, about 40 percent of the dancers are younger than 16. (The show is also popular with various art schools around the city, including the School of the Art Institute of Chicago.)

Austin says his inspiration for *Chic-A-Go-Go!* was a 1960s Chicago dance show, *Kiddie-A-Go-Go.* "The most appealing part was that it was live and not perfect," he says. "There's a charm about doing your best."

Everything about the show is free, or nearly so. Austin pays only $65 a year for the cable access, the production crew is volunteer, and the admission is free—they even serve free light refreshments. The only rule? That you dance and have fun.

They tape the shows at 322 South Green Street, a block west of Halsted, once a month, usually on a Saturday or Sunday afternoon. (Sign up for the e-mail list at chiclist@roctober.com to get notices of future taping dates, or visit their website at www.roctober.com.)

Prepare for a three-hour taping—they like to shoot two full shows, plus part of another show each time. And, if you like, bring a change of clothing for the different shows. The audience usually ranges from about 50 to 100 people—but they have never had to turn away anyone. The studio is near the University of Illinois El stop, and, if the parking gods are looking out for you, which is often the case on Saturday and Sunday afternoon in the west Loop, you may even be able to find street parking.

Chic-A-Go-Go! is good, simple fun—if your kids are young enough, they'll have a ball dancing to the music. If they're old enough to be embarrassed by their parents, they can go with friends or another trusted adult. It's like a club scene, without any of the worries.

Another bonus: Kids get to see how a television show is made—if they like, they can even volunteer to help out with production.

chicago international children's film festival

※ *Films screened at various locations in the city.*
Home theater is Facets Multimedia,
1517 W. Fullerton Avenue, Chicago, IL 60614
773-281-9075
Ideal Age Group: 2 to 18
Admission: $6
www.cicff.org

for budding spielbergs and coppolas

Do you have a young Spielberg in your household? Grab your popcorn and Junior Mints and reserve your seats for the annual Chicago International Children's Film Festival, held for 10 days each year, usually during late October. It was developed by Facets Multimedia, an independent movie and video emporium on Fullerton Avenue and one of the best movie resources in the country.

Facets began this festival in 1983 to introduce children to culturally diverse films. (Facets has a commitment to children's enlightenment—they began their children's programming, a precursor to the festival, as an antidote to violent Saturday morning cartoons.) It was the first competitive children's film festival in the U.S, and now it's the largest.

Each year approximately 25,000 kids, aged approximately 2 to 18, view the more than 200 live action and animated films, which are shown at different locations around the city—just like Chicago's film festival—such as the Biograph, or Facets itself. Directors, actors, producers, and Facets staff members lead before- and after-film discussions.

During the ten-day festival kids can also take part in special workshops, usually taught by a leading artisan, such as clay animation, stop motion, cinematography, acting, and creative writing. (These usually run about $15.00.)

Part of the fun of the festival is that Facets includes kids on the judging panels. Interested children must fill out a three-page application and go through an audition to first be accepted to either the Media Arts Camp or Young Chicago Critics, both of which qualify children to be judges. (These kids must be film buffs, though. They will watch approximately 75 films during the course of the festival.)

They also offer year-round programming for children that supports the festival and promotes the mission of film education, such as the aforementioned Young Chicago Critics, which teaches review writing and media literacy, and Facets Future Filmmakers, a program set up like a summer camp that teaches video and editing skills and storyboarding, and screens short films made by other children.

For out-of-towners, the festival offers special package deals that include discounted hotel rooms, restaurant coupons, and screening passes. For in- or out-of-towners, make sure you reserve your tickets early. Popular movies sell out.

chicago playworks

❉ *Merle Reskin Theatre, 60 E. Balbo Drive,*
Chicago, IL 60605
312-922-1999
Ideal Age Group: 5 to 12
Admission: Adults and children $8
http://theatreschool.depaul.edu/perform/playworks.php

big-time theater for little folks

This venerable theater is where professional Chicago actors take their kids. Founded as the Goodman's Children's Theatre in 1925, Chicago Playworks is the oldest continuously operating children's theater in Chicago (it was also the first theater to present a full planned season of performances for children in the United States). And it's under the auspices of the prestigious DePaul University's Theatre School. (At $8 a ticket, the price is right too.) The theater is close to public transportation, and offers discounted parking.

This association with the DePaul University makes for some special programming—not only do DePaul students get pre-professional experience, but Chicago's young audiences get to see some of the nation's top talent while it's still being nurtured. (Graduates of DePaul's Theatre School include Linda Hunt, Joe Montagna, and John C. Reilly.)

Part of what makes this theater so special, in addition to its prestigious history and long association with Chicago, is that it looks like grown-up theater! You get to come down to the Loop—the Merle Reskin Theatre is located in the blossoming South Loop—where million-dollar condos are going up across from Grant Park and new restaurants and coffee shops spring up daily. The structure is the old Blackstone Theatre, which seats 1325 (although they stop selling tickets at 900). With full productions, including sets, lights, and costumes, it looks and feels like a Broadway stage.

They try to keep the programming diverse and contemporary. Recent performances (which also include sign-language performances) have included *Ramona Quimby*, by perennial favorite Beverly Cleary. They also featured *The Highest Heaven* by Jose Cruz Gonzalez, the story of a young boy forced to return to Mexico during the Great Depression, and a version of *Pinocchio* with a high-tech twist.

Since the Merle Reskin Theatre is so conveniently located next to other Loop cultural destinations, some parents combine a trip to the Field Museum or Art Institute with the matinee. But if you like to sip your culture rather than gulp it, make it solely a theater day. Afterward, or before, walk several blocks west to historic Printer's Row and check out coffee shops, pizza parlors, and neighborhood pubs, which all serve lunch and dinner.

Savvy parents might want to check out the production guides that the theater publishes for each play. Primarily designed for teachers as learning aids in the classroom, they will mail you a copy before you come so you can discuss with your child the play's vocabulary, set design, costumes, and background. Ask for one when you make your reservation.

chicago public library

❊ *Main branch: 400 S. State Street, Chicago IL 60605*
312-747-4999
Ideal Age Group: All
Admission: Free
www.chicagopubliclibrary.org

books, fishing, and learning

Where can you learn to fish, bird-watch, get help with your homework, or visit Chicago's museums—all for free? Look no further than your local Chicago Public Libary branch—all 78 of them. While the national trend has been toward library budget cuts, Chicago has been on a rampage—building 32 neighborhood branches and renovating nine others in the past decade or so. The city plans to open 14 more branches by 2005. (They've even made it part of the city budget—a separate line funded by property taxes.)

In fact, the library branches offer a glimpse into the city itself. If Chicago is a city of neighborhoods, the branch libraries reflect this. The Humboldt Park Branch, with a large Latino population, has a generous Spanish-language collection. Uptown has collections in Vietnamese, Cambodian, and Chinese. The main branch, the awesome Harold Washington Library Center, opened a café for many of its empty-nester, post-suburban clientele.

In each branch, you'll find dynamite programs for kids, such as toddler and preschool programs that include storytelling, singing, dancing, puppet plays, and more. The libraries even offer vacation day specials, for those snowy or summer days when the kids need an outlet, and you've run out of ideas.

Older kids will find a range of programs, too. For example, kindergartners through eighth graders can join programs such as Dinosaur Detectives, or calligraphy classes, young writer's workshops, picture book brunch, even chess clubs. They can even take part in the annual Chicago Book Festival, which hosts adult and children programs in conjunction with other Chicago cultural institutions, such as multilingual fairy-tale readings, mother and daughter book clubs, or book-making for families.

Chicago kids can also take part in the Summer Reading Program, where they can earn t-shirts if they read enough books. All they have to do is report in to their local librarian—and no cheating!

And the library offers more than just intellectual pursuits. At 10 branches located near lagoons or branches of the Chicago River, including Sherman Park, Humboldt Park, and Rogers Park, you can use your library card to check out a fishing pole—and get instructions from a fishing expert. (They also provide a list of related fishing books.)

You can also check out their birding backpacks, complete with binoculars, an electric bird identifier, books, and a free journal. Or try the Get Wild About Reading backpack, which contains puzzles, books, and other activities. Are your kids stumped by homework? The library branches also offer free after-school tutoring by Chicago public school teachers-from Monday through Thursdays from 3 to 6 p.m.

Another library bonanza are the Great Kids Museum Passports, museum passes that adults can check out for one week that allow free admission to eleven area museums, including the Field Museum, the Chicago Children's Museum, the Adler Planetarium, and the Art Institute of Chicago. Each branch has several sets, so try another branch if yours is out.

chicago children's museum

❊ *700 E. Grand Avenue (Navy Pier),*
  Chicago, IL 60611-3428
  312-527-1000
  Ideal Age Group: Toddlers to 10
  Admission: Adults and children $7; seniors $6;
  children under one, free
  www.chichildrensmuseum.org

explore, climb, and create

This harum-scarum, three-story children's extravaganza fits perfectly into carnival-like Navy Pier, where the elegant Shakespeare Theater (see page 109) seems like an anomaly. Strolling up to this museum, you'll feel as though you're on the boardwalk in Atlantic City, without the Atlantic. You'll pass the vendors selling food and jewelry, you'll have a chance to ride a small train, or see a show at the I-Max Theatre.

Kids love this museum—originally begun as a few rooms in the Chicago Public Library. It's brightly painted, full of innovative and well-tended exhibits, and oriented toward play—it's especially appropriate for toddlers to 10-year-olds, although infants may enjoy a stroller view, and older kids can apprentice or volunteer.

They have great temporary exhibitions, such as a recent one on "Sesame Street," where kids can learn and play surrounded by familiar buildings and characters and even get a glimpse of what they'd look like on the show.

There are also 15 permanent exhibitions, such as the climbing schooner, for 5-year-olds and older—there was a long line when we were there—where kids can climb down a three-story ship, from crow's nest to deck. Treehouse Trails offers an array of make-believe forest for 5-year-olds and younger—they can camp out, climb a tree, play in a tree house, or crawl over giant logs.

The amazing Big Backyard is like a fantasy book come to life—kids get a bug's-eye view of the world—the flowers, toadstools, and insects tower over them, as they walk through this magical backyard (they can even try on insect wings).

There's also a construction site for industrious types. Waterways is for those who like to get their hands wet (you get to navigate your own boat down a "river," dealing with dams and locks). And you can even go on a dinosaur excavation—based on a 1997 Sahara dig that unearthed a never-before-seen species of dinosaur (a model of which stands in the museum).

All in all, there's enough at the museum to keep you busy for hours. You'll also find special events for each month, such as Chinese New Year celebrations, art classes, and music. City dwellers might also consider the museum for birthday parties, where you can rent a private party room and all day museum admission for guests. Or you can choose a step up and have a painting party or Super Chef party (where kids paint artistic pizzas).

However, be forewarned—some parents refer to this as a germ factory, so bring handiwipes, and prepare for some sensory overload: it's often crowded, noisy, and very stimulating.

If you need a break after all the fun, walk across the hallway from the entrance of the museum and visit the beautiful Crystal Garden, a one-acre indoor garden with 80 live palms and "leap-frog" fountains where the water seems to appear from nowhere. (Or of course, you can run outside and really get away from it all on the Pier's 150-foot-tall ferris wheel.)

chicago symphony center/kraft family matinee series

❄ *220 S. Michigan Avenue, Chicago IL 60604*
312-294-3000
Ideal Age Group: 5 to 12
Admission: Varies
www.cso.org

classical music for kids

One of Chicago's greatest treasures is the Chicago Symphony Orchestra which has won more than 50 Grammy Awards, made more than 900 recordings, and premiered more than 300 works, including the American debut of the Nutcracker Suite. The CSO is a big hit in Europe and Japan (sort of on par with Britney Spears), and some say it's the best orchestra in the world. The CSO's reputation may have hit its zenith with conductor Sir Georg Solti, but current conductor Daniel Barenboim is doing what few thought he could: carrying on the tradition.

Although primarily for adults, the CSO welcomes children 8 and older to its performances. What better way to introduce your child to great music? Symphony Center, the CSO's home since 1991, is spacious and beautiful, an appropriate complement to the music. Of course, even the most music-loving kid should be prepared: Each concert typically runs 2 hours, including intermission, and it helps a lot if they're familiar with the music. (Your best bet may be to use a CD to introduce your child to the particular pieces he or she will be hearing.)

For children younger than 8, the CSO offers the Kraft Family Matinee Series concerts. Recent performances have included a collaboration between CSO members and a local dance company that explored the different rhythms that make up the minuet, waltz, and mambo. Another featured trumpeter Wynton Marsalis exploring the roots of blues. Still another highlighted exotic Spanish orchestral works with accompanying dance styles, including flamenco. (You can order tickets online or by phone, but be warned: tickets go fast.)

Symphony Center offers Rhapsody Restaurant, a rather upscale establishment that may be fine for older kids, but for the young ones, stroll up or down Michigan Avenue to kid-friendly places such as Bennigan's, at 150 S. Michigan Avenue, or the Corner Bakery, at 224 S. Michigan Avenue. If you love great pizza and want to go a little downscale after the symphony, check out Chicago stalwart Exchequer at 226 S. Wabash.

children's humanities festival

❊ *Various city locations*
312-494-9509
Ideal Age Group: 5 to high school
Admission: $5 advance/$6 at the door
www.chfestival.org

art, music, poetry, and dance for young sophisticates

Don't blink or you'll miss this two-week fall event in Chicago—an offshoot of the amazing Chicago Humanities Festival, which is one of the best things about Chicago, and certainly one of the best-kept secrets. For two weeks each fall, nearly 45,000 Chicagoans race around the city to attend hundreds of music, drama, dance, literary, and political events all created around one theme, and all costing $5 or $6 at the door.

Now Chicago kids get the same treat. Approximately twenty programs over the two-week span encompass music, theater, storytelling, art workshops, and more. For example, past events featured R.L. Stine (creator of the popular *Goosebumps* series) creating new spooky stories with the audience, "Animation Station," a hands-on workshop to learn film animation, a poetry workshop led by a Pulitzer Prize–winning poet, and a master piano class for high schoolers.

The festival usually takes place during the last week of October and the first week of November at various Loop and Near North cultural centers, including the Harold Washington Library Center, the Sherwood Conservatory of Music, the Chicago Children's Museum at Navy Pier, and the DePaul Merle Ruskin Theatre. Tickets, which go on sale in September, sell quickly. So act fast. The best way to keep on your toes for these events is to get on the mailing list—or, better yet, become a Humanities Festival member or volunteer. You get advance notice, as well as discounts on tickets.

And don't fret if your kid's favorite author is in town and you forget to order the tickets. Since tickets are so reasonably priced, you always have a good chance that someone doesn't show up and you can buy a ticket at the door. (It worked for me at the grown-up festival for performances by Stephen Sondheim and Peter O'Toole.)

The Chicago Children's Humanities Festival is worth its weight in gold: It's a great way to introduce your kids to the arts and humanities without having to shell out big bucks for expensive summer camps or schools.

the children's museum of immigration

❊ *5211 N. Clark Street, Chicago, IL 60640*
773-728-8111
Ideal Age Group: 3 to 12
Admission: Adults $4; children and
seniors $3; children under 3 are free; $10 per family

cross the atlantic as an immigrant

This wonderful, compact museum is located on the third floor of the Swedish American Museum, at 5211 N. Clark St., in the heart of "Andersonville," Chicago's funky, hip, but still traditionally Swedish-American neighborhood. It's perfect for kids 3 to 12 who love a hands-on experience and for adults who also like to have a little education mixed in with fun. The museum is based on a role-playing exhibit developed in Sweden. Kids become part of an immigration story—starting on a farm in 1871 Sweden, and ending on the Minnesota prairie—all in the expanse of one big room.

You start with a guide—in our case 18-year-old Diana dressed in Swedish garb circa 1871—who will spin a pot lid that acts as a time machine, taking you all back in time with her, specifically to a Swedish farmhouse or "Stuga" where all the artifacts are authentic, either from Sweden, or Swedish-American families. Kids can don aprons and cook on the wood stove or climb into the trundle bed (where the parents slept upright and the kids were locked away in a cupboard overhead—which helps illustrate why these farmers longed for the New World). Kids also get a big kick out of the baby high chair-cum-potty, and the chamber pots that sit near the kitchen table. (Privacy, anyone?)

When you're done checking out the Swedish cabin, you can pack your trunk for your big journey. Diana recommended packing mostly food to sustain us on our long boat ride. Then you get to board the boat—a beautifully built wooden structure that allows you to walk to the hull and get a feel of the close quarters. (The exquisite murals painted by Swedish artists Lars Gillis help all this imaginary play.)

Passengers can take a turn at "rowing" the boat or standing on the deck to see if land's ahoy. When you alight in the New World, a farm in Minnesota, you can resettle in your new farm cabin. First, though, you may want to catch some fish for dinner with your magnetized fishing rod, ride a (wooden) horse, plant vegetables (velcroed onto the garden ground) or play some authentic pioneer games like wooden puzzles and blocks.

This cozy, neat, colorful exhibit is perfect for a rainy afternoon—and it's small and safe enough so that infants can crawl around and explore while older kids look around. Even high schoolers should enjoy this trip across the Atlantic.

When you're finished, stop by the first-floor museum store to check out children's books, holiday candles, and other treats. Or take a trip a few doors down to 5233 North Clark to Women & Children First Bookstore, where kids will find a wall of interesting and enlightening kids books. Of course, no trip to Andersonville is complete without a visit to Ann Sathers, the Chicago landmark Swedish restaurant, located several doors south of the museum, known for its cinnamon buns and home-cooked Swedish-American fare. Or you could walk across the street and down about a block to the famous Swedish Bakery at 5348 N. Clark Street—where the aromas alone are worth the trip.

the choo choo restaurant

✻ *600 Lee Street, Des Plaines, IL 60016*
847-391-9815
Ideal Age Group: 3 to 6
Admission: Meals average $6

lunch in a fifties diner

On the corner of Lee, Jefferson, and Park Place near downtown Des Plaines—about 20 miles northwest of downtown—
sits the Choo Choo Restaurant—a 1950s-style diner that features a model train that serves food.

This greasy-spoon for kids has been around for about 30
years in Des Plaines, which, although it has a newly rehabbed
downtown with condos and coffee shops, still holds onto its
kitschy 1950s feel, which makes it a perfect setting for the
Choo Choo, as the locals call it.

And this diner typifies kitsch. It's a small, one-room
restaurant, with booths surrounding a counter where a model
train rides along tracks on the countertop, delivering the
hamburgers, hot dogs, and grilled cheese sandwiches to its
young patrons.

Started in 1951 (parents who went there as kids now
take their own kids), the Choo Choo Restaurant was founded
by a WWII vet who dreamed of good old American fast food
when he was abroad. And when he returned, he built this
small diner. He also wore an engineer's cap and red bandanna, and blew a whistle whenever the train came through
with food. (Interesting trivia: In the 1950s, the Choo Choo
went head to head with another burger joint a few blocks
away—Ray Kroc's original McDonald's. Kroc paid the Choo
Choo a visit and told the owners not to worry: "I don't have
a place for people to sit down." So not only will your kids

love the hectic craziness of this little diner, but they'll be part of American fast-food history.)

Although no one now stands around in a cap and bandanna, today, much is the same at the Choo Choo. The young staff is friendly, patient, and helpful. The real fun for kids here is that they're kings and queens—they can sit at the counter by themselves while their parents sit behind them in booths. They mingle and talk to each other—it's like a big party or a kiddie bar.

It's noisy and rambunctious, and expect a line—especially on holidays or when school is out. So come early, and avoid federal holidays. (You'll also probably get to sing a happy birthday or two while you're there.) The menu is dirt cheap—kids meals run from about $3.95 for burger, fries, and a small drink to a whopping $4.10, if you add cheese to that burger. You can get a basketful of fries for under $2, and their milkshakes and root beer floats are just under $4. Most kids won't leave without the famous train cupcakes, complete with a train whistle on top.

Adults looking for some healthy fare can order veggie burgers and turkey chili, but, of course, you'll steal your kids' french fries and onion rings, so be prepared for a carb overload.

Here's a tip: Ahead of us in line, two grandparents had made a day trip out of the Choo Choo. They had parked their car up north on the Metra line and gave their grandson and granddaughter their first train rides, capped with a visit to the restaurant. It's a great idea—and you can do it from the city or the suburbs. The Des Plaines Metra train stops just a block away, and it's an easy walk, especially in the nicer weather.

dusable museum

❊ *740 W. 56th Place, Chicago, IL 60637*

773-947-0600

Ideal Age Group: 6 and up

Admission: Adults $3; students and seniors $2; children $1; children under 6, free

www.dusablemuseum.org

the country's best african-american museum

This Hyde Park treasure helps to give kids a more global understanding of the city's—and country's—history. The oldest, independent African-American history museum in the country, the DuSable was founded by Dr. Margaret Burroughs in 1961 (it moved to its current location in 1973).

Burroughs named the museum after Jean Baptiste Point DuSable, the first non-Native American settler of Chicago—and some say the city's true founding father. This majestic building overlooks Hyde Park's Washington Park—and is across the street from the University of Chicago Hospital. On the large front lawn, you'll find plenty of picnic tables and areas to sit. Keep this in mind if you go in seasonable weather—you can pack a lunch, or bring a blanket to enjoy the park. (The museum's expansion plans include a cafeteria; right now it has none.)

This museum has some wonderful permanent exhibits on the first floor, including Africa Speaks, a collection of African art, including bowls, masks, and sculptures. Don't miss the Slavery Room, which contains baptism dresses, washboards, and photos of slaves, signs listing rewards for runaway slaves and slave auctions, a model of a slave boat, and signs from segregation days reading "whites only." In this room, you'll also find signs appealing to "men of color" to strike, and information on the Illinois African-American soldiers who fought in the Civil War.

It's a graphic portrayal of America's segregationist history and a sobering reminder of how recently these laws and mores existed. (Caution: Some of the photos, specifically those of Klan lynchings and burnings, may be too graphic for young children.)

On the first floor you'll also find a replica of Harold Washington's mayoral office—complete with his framed law degree from Northwestern University. In order to capture his whole career, which included time as a U.S. Representative, the museum curators designed Washington's Chicago office to overlook the U.S. capitol. A rather surreal juxtaposition, but a great opportunity to talk to kids about the different branches of state and federal government.

Kids will love the basement exhibits, including a wonderful telling of the tale of the slave ship *Amistad*, where the "cargo" revolted and ended up on trial in America, where, eventually, some justice was served. You can read about the history of the boat, study maps, color in coloring books, and follow a timeline of the journey.

Art buffs can visit the permanent art collection, with paintings and sculptures by African-American artists. The museum also offers seasonal and visiting exhibits, including the annual Kwanzaa exhibit, which explains the seven principles and rituals of the holiday through videos, books, and a re-created Kwanzaa dinner.

A small gift shop near the entrance contains the usual museum goods: greeting cards, calendars, books, and T-shirts. It's a small museum, but filled with passion and history. As the guard said to me when I left, "We do African-American history year-round. People think it's only in February, but it's not."

the el

❖ *All over the city*

c/o the CTA: 888-YOUR-CTA

Admission: $1.50; children under 6, free

www.transitchicago.com

an insider's look at the city

This is the secret of urban parents stuck with unhappy kids on rainy or snowy days. Take them on a train ride! Chicago has one of the more historic public transportation lines in the country, the El (short for Elevated Railroad). While it's not always the most efficient mode of transport, it takes you through the heart of a great city. See the urban landscape. Hear the screeching wheels, the flickering lights. Ride it downtown, to one of the airports, around your neighborhood.

Where else in Chicago can you see the backs of brownstones, the tops of buildings, and the faces of your fellow city dwellers, all for a buck and a half (children under 6 ride free). It's a great opportunity for kids of all ages to just sit back and enjoy the ride. (And you'll be traveling the celluloid route seen in movies such as *Risky Business*, *The Fugitive*, and *The Blues Brothers*.)

As you ride the "El," tell the kids of its history: that the original system is more than 100 years old; that it was created by a lot of shady characters to serve the working people of Chicago; that it was an alternative to horse-drawn carriages, street cars, and cable cars. It was one of the first elevated trains in the country. (The submerged parts of the system didn't come along until the 1940s.) Listen to the announcements—most are automated now! And take turns reading the poetry and the ads on the walls.

You can sit right up front, near the motorman's car (they've phased out all conductors, and now these overworked motormen, or operators, must oversee the whole operation), or you can move around when the train stops. Buy a city map and follow where you're going as you get there. Look at the changing neighborhoods.

You might want to start with a special El ride, such as the CTA's Loop Tour Train, that takes you on a tour—for free! These forty-minute tours take place each Saturday afternoon, from May through September, with Chicago Architectural Foundation tour guides. As you ride along, they'll tell you the history of the Loop buildings and the El. (Pick up tickets at the Chicago Office of Tourism Visitor Information Center at 77 E. Randolph, or call 877-CHICAGO.)

Or, if it's between Thanksgiving and Christmas, hop aboard the Holiday Train, a garishly decorated car (with hand poles trussed up in red and white, holiday music, and garland and lights) staffed by elves who give out candy canes. (A recent holiday car derailed and everyone had to be evacuated, even Santa. But all were safe.)

Another fun El ride is the Haunted El, around Halloween, which transforms the Orange Line into a haunted mansion, with a local theater troupe providing the mostly tame ghost stories. All this for the regular $1.50 fare.

If you just want to do the El thing yourself, you might consider riding the Brown Line (all the El trains now are color-coded), which takes you from Ravenswood into the Loop. This line is almost entirely elevated, and it's nice and curvy, winding around buildings that were constructed after the El tracks. On its brief street-level leg of the journey, you can see quaint houses and go over the Chicago River.

For those who live up north, the Purple Line starts in Wilmette and runs through Evanston, taking you through the tree-lined neighborhoods and downtown space where you can see the full range of shops, homes, and businesses.

The CTA's newest line, the Orange Line, takes you from the Loop to the refurbished Midway Airport (which even

Madonna now flies into). It circles the Loop clockwise before heading south to the airport. You'll find lots of criss-crossing and parallel tracks on this line, which makes it great fun for train buffs.

The best part about the El is that it takes no pre-planning and it's always available. Be prepared, however: Stations are not particularly stroller-friendly, and you may not want to schlep strollers, kids, and bags up some of the stairs.

exploratorium, skokie:

❋ *4701 Oakton St., Skokie, IL 60076*
847-674-1500, ext. 2700
Ideal Age Group: 0 to 8
Admission: Adults $2; children $5; children under 2, $2 .
Discounts for Skokie residents
www.skokieparkdistrict.org

an indoor playground!

If you travel to Skokie, a suburb just north of the city, you'll hit a kid trifecta—three cool places within shouting distance of each other: The Exploratorium, a huge, indoor playground; the Skokie Water Playground, a great array of water slides and pools; and Emily Oakes Nature Center, 13 acres of peaceful prairie. .

Let's start with the Exploratorium, an indoor playground that will hold the attention of infants to 8-year-olds—especially on rainy or cold days when you've run out of ideas. Children can get their pent-up-inside-too-long ya-yas out running around the large basement-level playground. It's like a big kindergarten room without any rigid school rules.

In one section, kids will have a blast playing diva in a wonderful mock theater, complete with backstage stage mirrors and lighting, a trunk of costumes, and a stage on which to perform.

You'll also find the requisite computer station with educational computer games, and a large art area with everything a would-be artist needs to let loose—paints, smocks, colored pencils, crayons, and papers. There's a water play area, and even small trucks and scooters for the really young ones.

The pièce de résistance, however, is the two-and-a-half story climber, complete with slides, tunnels, and swaying bridges. It's a climber's dream. Linda, one of the Exploratorium staff, said that one of the best things about this playground—which is often rented out for birthday parties—is that "you can't lose your child."

It's a lot more low-key than some of the splashier kids' museums in Chicago, without a café or other frills. If you're really hungry, you can venture into the small vending machine room, but most parents, Linda said, take a break for lunch—your entry fee is good for the entire day.

Of course, if you're visiting in the summer, few kids will let you get away without checking out the adjacent outdoor Skokie Water Playground, an awesome array of 120-foot waterslides, zero-depth pools, baby pools, sprinklers, and sand playgrounds that most kids from all over the area know and revere. (You'll pay a separate entrance fee.)

The Exploratorium and waterslide are also about half a mile from the Emily Oaks Nature Center at 4650 Brummel—13 acres of peaceful Illinois Oak savanna, with a paved hiking path that offers a touch of nature in this congested suburb. When I was there on an unseasonably warm October day, the other few walkers were cheerful and friendly—and the park district workers were hanging the holiday lights on the trees for the annual holiday light show.

Skokie is conveniently located on the North Side of the city for those who live in the northern suburbs or who have access to Eden expressway. (Deli lovers take note: Skokie is also home to Kaufman's Deli at 4905 Dempster Street, about a mile north, home to some of the best bagels around.)

the field museum of natural history

❃ *1400 S. Lake Shore Drive, Chicago, IL 60605-2496*
312-922-9410
Ideal Age Group: 5 to 17
Admission: Adults $10; children ages 3–11, $5;
seniors and students $7
www.fieldmuseum.org

dinosaurs, mummies, and more!

Home of the famous dinosaur Sue, the Field Museum of Natural History—founded in 1893 to house the biological and anthropological collections assembled for the World's Fair–is now part of Chicago's Lakefront Museum Campus, which also includes the Shedd Aquarium and Adler Planetarium.

The Field Museum was a destination for many Chicago kids even before the huge T. Rex graced its grounds. (Nearly everyone who grew up in Chicago can recall the annual field trip to the Museum.) It also has an amazing mummy exhibition, world-class information on Native American culture, and cool nature stuff. (Lots of gory stuff that kids love, but grounded in history, natural and otherwise.)

But we have to start with Sue, the largest, most complete T. Rex ever found—it's about 90 percent complete, and 67 million years old. Kids can learn how it took two years for Field technicians to clean away the mud and rock from her bones, as well as what else goes on behind the scenes at the museum when they visit the museum's Fossil Preparation Laboratory.

Kids also love the mummy display in the Inside Ancient Egypt exhibit, where they can visit the replica of a tomb that contains actual carvings excavated from a real tomb. You can also see how mummies were made (and why), as well as walk along a Nile marsh and experience life in ancient Egypt.

Another popular exhibit is the Lions of Tsaro—two taxidermied man-eating lions from East Africa, each measuring nearly 10 feet from head to tail, that terrorized an English railroad project. The lions killed more than 140 workers before they were stopped. You can learn natural and man-made history with such exhibits.

Smaller kids may love the Underground Adventure, which is about, in a word, dirt. You get to see what it would be like to be about 1/100 of your regular size and walk through the soil where you'll see the now-huge critters, including june beetles and oribatid mites, that populate the dirt's neighborhood. You also get to see what grows in the subterrain, including fungi, seeds, and spores.

In the outstanding Native American halls you can learn about the day-to-day lives and culture of many North American tribes, including those of the Eskimos to tribes in Mexico and Central America.

The Field Museum also hosts an array of special programming, much of it for children, such as classes on the Field scientists' latest research, collaborations with local theater troupes such as Redmoon in celebration of natural history, and storytelling. You can also take part in some of the best family field trips ever—look good without having to do the work—by tagging along to Chinatown or nearby Mazon Creek where the real-life archaeologists learn about ancient Illinois.

You can even sleep overnight at the museum—if the mummies don't scare you! It's called Dozin' with the Dinos, and you can explore Ancient Egypt by flashlight and spread out your sleeping bag in the middle of some of your favorite exhibits.

The museum hosts many special, temporary exhibits (admission to them often costs an extra fee). Check the website for upcoming events, and buy your tickets early.

The Field Museum has worked hard to make this rather intellectual natural history treasure a kid destination, and it's working. It's also accessible. CTA buses stop right out front, you can walk from the Loop if you don't mind a mini-trek, or you can pay $12 in the nearby parking garage.

Prepare to spend several hours there and assume you'll work up an appetite. They offer McDonald's and the Corner Bakery, although you might be best off just packing a picnic lunch. The Field Museum is a place to rediscover again and again—but let the kids call the shots. They can become archaeologists all on their own.

garfield park conservatory

✳ *300 N. Central Park Avenue, Chicago, IL 60624*

312-746-5100 for general information;

773-638-1766 for classes and programs

Ideal Age Group: 2 to 12

Admission: Free (including parking)

www.garfield-conservatory.org

a tropical rain forest on the west side

This long-overlooked gem—the nearly 100-year-old Garfield Park Conservatory—is nestled on Chicago's once grand West Side, whose boulevards and greystones are now being restored from dilapidation. The conservatory has also recently undergone a rebirth of sorts—the whole thing has been refurbished and the city keeps adding more buildings and attractions. (In fact, the city is making this small section of the West Side into a green haven—with solar-powered buildings and sustainable businesses.)

The conservatory itself is the largest public conservatory in the United States, with nearly two acres of greenery under grass, all in natural settings—the first in the country to do so. You can get there easily by car—and parking's free—or it's right off the Lake Street El, at a beautifully refurbished, ornate stop that looks like an extension of the conservatory.

Inside the conservatory itself, you'll find a maze of rooms, including the Palm House that houses the largest under-glass palm in the world; the Fern Room, a taste of paradise, complete with a waterfall and goldfish pond (I had to drag the friend who I came with from this tropical beauty); the Sweet House, with coffee and berry plants; and the amazing Desert House with cacti that resemble aliens perched on a moonscape.

This leads right into the Children's Gardens—an area with a spongy ground surface on which kids can run, crawl, and explore. There's a toddler play area, a large sculpture of a seed, and lots of cool plants, such as the firecracker plants and the powder puff trees. There's even a second floor with a pretty adventurous slide that twists and turns back to the ground floor. The staff is extremely friendly, helpful and welcoming. It's obvious that they tend to these gardens—and the kids who come here—with much care.

Garfield Park also offers special exhibits for kids. One recent exhibit features towering skeletons, ancient fossils, and artists' renderings of dinosaurs set amid the plants. Seasonal flower shows are the norm, as are seasonal programs. Check out the County Fair, with pony rides and face painting, the Chocolate Fest—where you can see the harvest from Chicago's only fruiting chocolate trees, and the seasonal concerts. You can also take advantage of the Children's Garden's free weekend activities, find out how to get rubbings of your favorite plants, or carve pumpkins at Halloween.

If you come in the summer, make a day of it and visit the Garfield Park Market. Open on Saturdays and Sundays, this San Francisco–type open air market sells vegetables, arts, and crafts.

While you're in the neighborhood, make sure to visit the Peace Museum, which is housed in the nearby Garfield Park Conservatory (you can't miss its gold dome). The Peace Museum (773-638-6450; www.peacemuseum.org), which is located on the second floor, is the only museum in the country that explores the impact of war and peace through the arts. Kids can read books, color, and create their own posters, all around the theme of peace.

gilson park

❊ *Lake and Michigan Avenue, Gilson Park, IL*
847-256-9656
Admission: Free during winter; in the summer parking
decal required. M–F $5; Sat. and Sun. no parking
www.wilmettepark.org

a free, lakefront haven

One of the prettiest stretches of beachfront land can be found
just north of Evanston—about 14 miles north of the Loop—in
Wilmette's Gilson Park. Chicago natives often take this 60-
acre sprawl of park for granted. On nearly any day that you
visit there—except for holidays and special events—most of
your fellow park-goers are Chicago's immigrants, who often
have a fresher perspective on Chicago's gems.

You can picnic, bicycle, walk, play soccer or tennis here,
along with hanging out at several great playgrounds. Bring
your beach toys and buckets—although swimming is allowed
only in the adjacent, lifeguarded Gilson Beach which costs
$6.50 a day for non-residents. The wide expanse of clean
sand is great to play in.

Another treat is a beautiful walking path that winds down
to the harbor, where you can sit on benches and look at the
boats and seagulls. There's also a long, rocky point that juts
out into the lake, with lots of scary big waves crashing on it—
a great adventure for slightly older kids under the watchful
eye of an adult.

In the summertime, you may decide to come up for a
free concert (these are usually held on Thursday, Friday, and
Saturday nights) at Gilson Park's Wallace Bowl, an outdoor
Greek-style amphitheater that hosts a series of opera, jazz,
pop, and country western concerts—most performed by local

bands and orchestras. They always feature one extravagant Broadway musical each summer, and past efforts have included the *Music Man* and *Singing in the Rain*. These concerts and performances are perfect for kids—they can run around, be noisy at times, eat, and no one really cares. It's like one huge family-reunion picnic. Dancing in the aisles is permitted.

As an added bonus, when you visit Gilson Park, leave time to walk across Sheridan Avenue to the Bahai Temple—the world headquarters of the Bahai faith—a sort of ecumenical religion with roots in the Middle East that was founded in the 19th century. The Bahai's emphasis on unity and peace is evident in this soaring temple made from steel, cement, and white quartz. Finished in 1953 (it took a total of 50 years to build, what with fires and stops and starts), this building has nine entrances—a cool thing to count with your kids—representing the world's different faiths. The sanctuary itself is awesome—a soaring ceiling topped by a dome.

Downstairs you can find out more about the Bahais—but the real fun for kids may be the lush gardens that surround the Temple—kids can throw coins in the fountains, walk through the garden mazes, or climb the grand front stairs that lead into the main sanctuary. If you go in summer, you'll be sure to run into wedding parties getting their pictures taken against the temple's backdrop, and tourists from around the world.

grant park

❃ *Bounded by Randolph Drive, Roosevelt Road, Michigan Avenue, and Lake Michigan*

c/o Chicago Park District: 312-742-PLAY

Ideal Age Group: 2 to teen

Admission: Free

www.chicagoparkdistrict.com

a free field for music, walking, and playing

Grant Park is like the ultimate playground for Chicago parents—it's big, it's free, and it's full of things that kids love. It's bounded by Randolph Drive on the north, Roosevelt Road on the south, Michigan Avenue on the west, and Lake Michigan on the east. (Basically, it's between the Loop and the Lake.) Built on the landfill of debris from the Great Fire of 1871, its 220 acres contain elm trees, rose gardens modeled after those at Versailles, a prairie wildflower garden, and lots of hidden treasures.

Let's start with Buckingham Fountain—an enduring symbol of Chicago that every kid needs to play in at least once. Then you can check out the outdoor summer concerts at the Petrillo Music Shell (many of them free), which include the Chicago Blues Festival, Chicago Jazz Festival, and the Chicago Gospel Festival. (Taste of Chicago is also held here, but you have to be pretty devoted to gorging to make it through the crowds with kids in tow.) You can join the thousands of Chicagoans who bring blankets, picnics, and even candles and sit back on a summer evening and let the kids run along the grass. (A perennial summer favorite is the Grant Park Music Festival, a series of free concerts by the Chicago Symphony Orchestra.)

You can also take long walks in the Park—perhaps even

over to the south end of Grand Park near Balboa and Colum-
bus Drives in the summer to watch the home of Chicago-style
16-inch softball.

If you want more action, check out the north side
of Grant Park, Daley Bicentennial Plaza, located above the
Monroe Street Parking Garage, where you can ice skate in the
Loop—it's the first ice rink in downtown Chicago and host to
some shots from the television series "ER"—for merely $2 a
skate for adults, $1 for kids. (Skate rentals are cheap, too—
just $2.) It's sublime to skate in nature by the tall downtown
buildings. The rink is open approximately from November
through March (weather permitting), and in the summer it
becomes a stage, a roller-skating rink, or just a hanging out
place, depending on the day. Don't miss the annual Winter-
fest, which usually takes place in February, for ice-skating,
carriage rides, and hot chocolate. In warmer weather, walk a
few blocks to the Green, an 18-hole miniature golf course
open April through October. There are also picnic tables and
12 chess tables.

No description of Grant Park would be complete without
mention of the brand new Millennium Park—while not
officially a part of Grant Park, it's close enough to make it a
kissing cousin. Ultimately, this 24.5-acre park-within-a-park
will contain gardens, a performing arts pavilion, and land-
scaped walkways.

the grove

❊ *1421 Milwaukee Avenue, Glenview, IL 60025*

847-299-6096

Ideal Age Group: Infant to 12

Admission: Free

www.glenviewparkdist.org

preserved prairie and creepy crawlies

In the middle of the strip malls in north suburban Glenview, you'll find the Grove, 124 acres of preserved prairie and pioneer-era buildings on Milwaukee Avenue, which is actually on an old stagecoach line.

Today, the Grove is a National Historic Landmark run by the Glenview Park District. It was originally the land of Dr. John Kennicott, a Louisiana-born physician and horticulturist who moved northward with his family and staked his claim on a patch of "grove," or shady land in the middle of the open prairie. Today, about 150 years later, it's a kids' haven, complete with indigenous animals, insects, and plants. (Since the Grove is a park district offering, admission for visiting the lands and the animals is free—as is the ample parking.) The Grove's Natural Science Classroom—a building that houses the indoor creatures and educational center—is open to visitors every day until 4:30 p.m.

In this nature center you'll find owls, frogs, and turtles—including a 100-year-old turtle that comes to the top of the tank for a breath of air about once an hour—along with fish and snakes that are indigenous to Illinois waters. Little kids love this place, and even slightly older ones get into the exotic bugs, including the hissing Madagascar cockroaches, which the cheerful staff will take out of their tank for you. (A bop on the head incites them to hiss.) Kids can also study various snakes, watch nature movies, do puzzles, or read books. It's interactive, self-guided, and relaxed. (Kids won't hear much "Do not touch" around here.)

Outside, you can take a self-guided tour on the two-mile walking path through prairie, wetlands, and oak woodlands, where you might see (or hear) redheaded woodpeckers and orioles, and see (in spring and summer) Michigan Lily, Prairie Phlox, Prairie Dock, and Spiderwort. You can also pack a lunch, as picnic tables are available in designated areas.

Interested in history? Visit the log cabin and the Native American village, which includes a tipi. Or tour Doctor Kennicott's 1856 house and see where the doctor and his family (and servants) once churned butter and wove cloth for the children's clothing.

The Glenview Park District hosts special events at the Grove throughout the year for reasonable prices (admissions range from free to $6 for adults and $1 per child). You're likely to find crowds on these days, so get there early, and expect to bump into other folks enjoying the day. Past events have included a Civil War reenactment (the participants are so into it, they don't break character once!); a folk fest with live music, barn dancing, and nature walks; a pumpkin fest with hayrides; and the Owl Prowl—where nature buffs can walk the trails of the park looking for owls in the wild, and study more about them back at the nature center.

It's no wonder that thoughtful parents, grandparents, aunts, uncles, and other special adults in children's lives make good use of the Grove—I know one grandfather who takes his grandson there once a week. The Grove is a good embodiment of the French phrase "Plus ca change, plus c'est la meme chose"— "the more things change the more they stay the same." This timeless exhibit of nature will help kids use their imaginations to picture life before strip malls, Chuck E. Cheese, and the Internet. They may also start to feel a kinship with Illinois' native plants and animals.

chicago's 50 best places to take children

health world children's museum

❄ *1301 S. Grove Avenue, Barrington, IL 60010*

847-842-9100

Ideal Age Group: 5 to 14

Admission: Adults and children $6; children under 2, free

www.healthworldmuseum.org

belching, brains, and other health-related exhibits

Interested in bodily functions? Then you won't want to miss this behemoth health museum nearly an hour's drive from downtown in northwest suburb Barrington. (You'll know you're there by the sea of minivans in the huge parking lot.)

In fact, the museum's hit section, Grossology, the (Impolite) Science of the Human Body, features a human skin climbing wall (with warts and all!); a "burp machine" that shows the audio effect of built-up acid indigestion; and a life-size "Operation" game, where kids can play surgeon and remove organ parts from a human body. There's also a vomit center, and the scoop on poop.

However, all is not body fluids and odors. This is the nation's first health-learning museum—debuting nearly 10 years ago. The 85,000-square-foot resource is designed for kindergartners through 8th graders.

It's large and colorful, and as soon as you walk through the front door, you'll be drawn to the hands-on exhibits. For example, you can test your flexibility with machines that measure how close you can get to touching your toes, or keep your balance. You can also find out your height and weight. Or climb through a human heart. (Be prepared: the loud music in some of the exhibits reminds me of the O'Hare United Terminal.)

Kids can also play doctor or nurse in the Health Village, with a simulated emergency room, dentist, and doctor's office. (It comes complete with an ambulance.) You can also sit through the 25-minute Brain Theater, which takes you through a multimedia exhibit of human brain activities; watch a younger-set video on the five senses; or, somewhat randomly, tour a Metra train stuck in the middle of the exhibit, with a 15-minute video on railroad safety.

For budding environmentalists, there's the Oak Forest, an indoor woodland featuring a two-foot-high treehouse and gigantic fish tank. For more passive pursuits, they have a library resource center, with books, magazines, and audiovisual materials. If you need a break from the belching belly and other loud noises, they also offer an art center where you can (quietly) draw and paint.

The museum's mission is to "promote health education and provide children with the information they need to build healthy lives," and most of this is done with great fun and imagination. However, at times it feels a little like a science class—slightly didactic and preachy (they have a cast of characters such as Susie the Sneeze, Barefoot Bob, and Louie the Louse who—gasp!—uses dirty combs). Also, you won't find any alternative health exhibits here.

However, you will find lots to keep you occupied for several hours. If you get hungry, you can get (ironically, rather unhealthy) lunches at Georgi's Garden Café, or bring your own snacks. They have a picnic area. (You're not near any other restaurants or shops, so it's pretty much a one-destination trip.)

But while you're out there, ask about their special birthday and group events.

indian boundary park

❊ *2500 W. Lunt Avenue, Chicago, IL 60645*

312-742-7887

Ideal Age Group: 2 to 12

Admission: Free

www.chicagoparkdistrict.com

a zoo, a playground, and cultural center

This West Rogers Park play area has been making kids happy since the 1920s. Nestled among the increasingly gentrified neighborhood, long the home to Chicago's orthodox Jewish community, this large piece of city land has it all for urban kids—a sprinkler park, a mini-zoo, volleyball field, lots of room for running around and playing catch, and an awesome playground.

If you enter the park on Lunt Avenue, pass through two stone columns where kids sometimes perch like gargoyles. That's the beauty of this park. It provides enough structure for those kids who need it and enough freedom for more imaginative ones.

Some of this imagination will take flight in the offerings of the immaculately maintained Indian Boundary Cultural Center—check out the faces carved into the wood beams! There is a series of free concerts by the Chicago Civic Orchestra, the training orchestra for the Chicago Symphony. All of the concerts are interactive and family-oriented, including one specifically for children.

You'll also find a host of classes, mostly for kids ages 6 to 12. Since this is a cultural center, the classes center around the arts, including theater, improvisation, piano, voice, sculpture, painting, and dance. There's even a kids' yoga class. Classes aren't free, but they're so nominally priced—about a buck a class—they might as well be. (For more sports-oriented classes, check out Warner Park, 312-742-7888, just four blocks away, that has a skating rink and skateboard park.)

Outside, right behind the Cultural Center, is the Indian Boundary Lagoon, a one-acre pond with a small island and a weeping willow tree. Even in the winter, the Lagoon is beautiful—with native prairie grasses, and a few ducks still skating around the frozen surface. Next to the Lagoon is a large concrete area with a sprinkler pole in the middle for summer water play—remember to bring your bathing suit! (And a picnic lunch—you'll find ample picnic tables, or, if you'd prefer, walk the few blocks to Western Avenue and have ice cream and popcorn at Jacky's ice cream parlor. Or drive south a bit to Devon Avenue for Indian all-you-can-eat lunch buffets.)

The all-wood playground offers creative play opportunities and it's a beauty—the spires of the wooden structures echo the spires of the surrounding 1920s brick apartment and condominium buildings—all connected with tunnels, bridges, and climbing poles. My young guide loved the tire tunnel—which burrowed deep in the sand, the "wobbly" bridges, the train, and the forts built into the structure.

If you prefer more "wild" entertainment, about 50 feet from the playground is the Indian Boundary Zoo—the only other zoo in Chicago's borders besides Lincoln Park Zoo. It houses an intimate collection of animals that includes Beth the cow; brown, white, and rust-colored llamas, sheep, swans, and lots of different birds in a separate bird sanctuary peppered with bird houses. (See if you can come during feeding time, or read up about these animals before you go to the park.)

Indian Boundary Park also has lots of play area—tennis courts, basketball courts, and a sand volleyball area. Kids can also run, play catch, and have races on the wide-open fields. There's not a lot not to like about Indian Boundary Park. It's a Chicago classic.

jackson park/
japanese gardens

❋ *6401 S. Stony Island, Chicago, IL 60649*
312-747-6187
Ideal Age Group: 4 to 12
Admission: Free (but depends on activity or program)
www.chicagoparkdistrict.com

zen calm in hyde park

Do you crave some quiet in your day? Want to teach the kids in your life about some counter-cultural stuff (read: non-hyper activity?). Come to Hyde Park's Jackson Park—a large city park that encompasses a field house, acres and acres of wooded land, and this exquisite jewel, long the secret of Hyde Parkers—the Osaka Japanese Stroll Garden, located directly south of the Science and Industry Museum. (Or need a breather after your hectic day in the Museum? Stroll the quarter mile to this sanctuary.) You can take the #10 bus from downtown or drive and park at the Science and Industry's parking lot or find street parking west of Jackson Park.

The gardens are located against the backdrop of the University of Chicago's ivy-covered buildings to the west, and a small lagoon to the east, and the Science and Industry to the north. (Bring your camera or sketch pad. It's a great view of the city.)

Originally a gift from Japan for the 1893 World's Fair, a fire eventually destroyed the gardens, which were restored in 1995 after the mayor of Osaka, Japan, donated a traditional Japanese garden entrance gate. Today, it's part of the Chicago Park District, which tends to it with the help of dedicated volunteers.

The gardens are a major chill pill for children. Not only can they commune with nature, in the form of beautiful plants and flowers, but they can walk over the small bridge, play in the tea ceremony shelter, or climb the large stones near the lagoon. It's a perfect place for play dates, picnic lunches, or reading or coloring on a spring or summer day.

Even though you're smack in the middle of the city here, you feel a sense of small community. For example, on a recent fall day, a photographer was taking a family portrait, an extended family was out for a Sunday stroll, and a young woman was practicing yoga in the sheltered teahouse.

As an added treat, each September the city hosts the annual (and free) Osaka Garden Festival, where you can taste different foods in A Taste of Japan, attend musical performances, and check out some martial arts. They also have a tea ceremony.

If you're a non-Hyde Parker, once you're in the area, look around. This is Chicago's oldest suburb—established in the mid-1800s. A range of notable architects designed many of the beautiful greystones and Victorian houses. The influence of the University of Chicago is strong—it's where the atom was split, Mike Nichols and Elaine May got started, and where Indiana Jones-like archaeologist Paul Serveno works.

It's also host to a million other interesting restaurants, parks, and museums, including, of course, the Science and Industry, but also the Oriental Institute Museum of the University of Chicago, where kids can learn about ancient Egypt (including preparing a mummy for burial), and the Smart Museum of Art, the art museum of the University of Chicago where you can stop by on Wednesday afternoons during the summer from noon to 3 p.m., and kids can take part in free art classes, as long as they are accompanied by an adult.

kohl children's museum of greater chicago

❊ *165 Green Bay Road, Wilmette, IL 60091*

847-512-1300

Ideal Age Group: 0 to 8

Admission: Adults and children 6$; seniors 5$;

children under 1, free

www.kohlchildrensmusuem.org

where the under-8 crowd goes to have fun

This North Shore favorite—located on Green Bay Road in Wilmette—offers much of what Navy Pier's Chicago's Children's Museum does, without the hassle of parking and overwhelming crowds.

One of the selling points of this amazing cornucopia of goodies is that they aim to please the birth through eight-year-old crowd only. While that means a lot of noise and running around, there's very little text to wade through at each exhibit and each exhibit is geared toward interactive play. You can almost see the brain cells developing before your eyes.

For example, they have an amazing music exhibit where kids can beat bongos in a sound-proof room, compose music via computer, create images on a screen with their dancing bodies, and play disc jockey by creating a track with melody, harmony, and rhythm. We saw several young composers and DJs hard at work.

Or there's the Great Kohl Sailing Ship—part cargo ship, part fishing vessel—where kids can "catch" fish, raise and lower the sail, load cargo into the hold, or I suppose, pretend to be Johnny Depp in *Pirates of the Caribbean*. Carrying on with the water theme, the H_2O exhibit allows kids to get their hands—and clothes!—wet.

For grocery store buffs, kids can be clerks, or patrons at a mini-Jewel/Osco grocery store complete with shopping carts, fully stocked shelves, and check-out clerk aprons. When I was there, two young boys were seriously discussing the price of milk with a little girl "patron." In fact, the kids at the museum interact well with each other—these museums may be the closest thing we have these days to a community playground.

Bob the Builder fans can help build a nearly full-sized house—the already existing wooden frame can be added to with blocks, wheelbarrows, and pulleys—a bit like Sisyphus rolling the rock up the hill just to have it roll back again, but a big hit with the kids. You can also "ride" a real CTA car and even add sound effects by pushing buttons that play recorded train noises and conductor announcements (for those who don't get enough of that during the week). There's a computer station with educational software. Upstairs is a more mellow art scene, where kids can draw, paint, and take art classes.

The museum features lots of monthly special programs and exhibits as well. For example, in November, you can make corn prints with paint and corncobs, or create and decorate musical instruments with corn kernels and recycled containers. Recently, they hosted a wonderful Maurice Sendak tribute exhibit, where kids slid into "chicken soup with rice" or really puffy Styrofoam.

Although this museum is lots of fun—the level of stimulation is high. Be prepared. Don't pack a lot else into your day when you come here, and make sure you have adequate quiet time before and after. (Note: This current building was not constructed as a museum, which explains part of the noise issue. However, the Kohl Museum is in the process of building a custom-designed space in Glenview—a suburb directly west of Wilmette—into which they'll move in October 2005. The new space will be much larger and, they hope, quieter, with nooks located throughout for nursing mothers or those who just need a time out.)

lambs farm

❈ *14245 Rockland Rd., Libertyville, IL 60048*
847-362-4636
Ideal Age Group: 3 to 6
Admission: Adults $5; children $10
www.lambsfarm.org

This 70-acre farm in suburban Libertyville offers families a chance to support a nonprofit organization dedicated to the growth and well-being of those with developmental disabilities. They've combined this with the opportunity to visit with farm animals, play miniature golf, and take part in other rides and activities in a beautiful pastoral setting.

When they founded Lambs Pet Store in Chicago, co-owners Bob Terese and Corinne Owen employed 12 developmentally disabled adults to help serve customers and take care of the animals. Their store's mission soon won many admirers, including Chicago philanthropist W. Clement Stone, who donated his Libertyville farm to the cause. In 1965, Lambs Farm opened.

The premise is simple: By affording dignity and training to those with disabilities, everyone comes out ahead. To this end, the Farm serves as a residential and training facility for more than 250 disabled adults. In addition to the training that they receive on campus, they also help to run Aunt Mary's Country Store, where they sell jams, jellies, pasta sauces, and pastries, all made from scratch, or the Country Inn Restaurant, open for breakfast and lunch.

Vintage lovers can shop at the Lambs Thrift Shop, which sells men's, women's, and children's clothing, furniture, toys and books. Or stop by the Pet Shop (discuss possible purchases with your kids ahead of time!) to check out the puppies, kittens, birds, and lizards. They also offer compassionate dog training to those with problem pups.

The real treats for kids include the Discovery Center, where kids can pet and learn about farm animals, and the Farmyard, where a collection of ponies, donkeys, chickens, and pigs keep kids thrilled and curious. (They get to be up-close-and-personal with many of these animals.) They can also, for small fees, ride the carousel, the miniature train (little kids love this!), or play an 18-hole miniature golf course.

Plan to bring snacks and handiwipes.

the lincoln park conservatory

❊ *2391 N. Stockton Drive, Chicago, IL*
773-742-7736
Ideal Age Group: 5 to 10
Admission: Free
www.chicagoparkdistrict.com

a green respite in the city

A close neighbor of the Lincoln Park Zoo and Peggy Note-baert Nature Museum, this beautiful, 80-plus-year-old plant and flower sanctuary provides kids with a place to see nature—everything from green, blooming plants to the prickly cacti of the desert. They have wonderful seasonal shows—a myriad of poinsettias at Christmas, for example, or Easter lilies during the spring.

The Lincoln Park Conservatory is not an entire-afternoon trip, but it's stroller friendly, and it provides a wonderful rest stop, or addendum to a day at Lincoln Park Zoo. This is another Chicago Park District effort—and they've done a wonderful job of preserving this dewdrop of nature. Built between 1890 and 1895, this conservatory is a product of Victorian interest in horticulture. (The whole place has a very Victorian feel—elegant and refined. They have benches placed strategically in each room, and you almost expect to see a few handkerchiefs or two next to them.)

Today, the grand entry room is the palm house—50 feet high in the center—with more than two dozen palm trees from around the world. It's peaceful and warm—and smells good, too, and can restore sanity to parents and kids cooped up too long during a Chicago winter. Check out the Storks at Play fountain.

The fern room is next, looking like a prehistoric landscape—before Illinois was a prairie, it was a wet, tropical forest—and they have cycad ferns, among the oldest species of plants, surviving since dinosaur times. This will thrill the young kids, and provide adults with a teachable moment. Also look for the 50-foot high fiddle leaf rubber tree.

The next room, the Orchid House, has a goldfish pond—but no coin-throwing here, unfortunately! Instead, pack colored pencils or crayons and see how many colors of the plants, flowers, and fish you can capture on paper.

The final room in this all-too-brief sojourn contains whatever special exhibit is featured at the time—the mums during the fall, poinsettias during Christmastime, and lilies during spring. Whoever arranges the plants and flowers does so with a discerning eye—the colors and arrangements are prettier than most any garden around. (Young artists can create masterpieces here, too.)

All of this, of course, is free. Lincoln Park Conservatory might work best for kids still young enough to enjoy a simple outing with mom, dad, or a grandparent. It also may be the perfect way to calm down kids too used to computer games and over-stimulation. It's a place to walk, observe, and just be.

lincoln park zoo

❊ *2001 N. Clark Street, Chicago, IL 60614*
312-742-2000

Ideal Age Group: 2 to 12

Admission: Free

www.lpzoo.com

the best free zoo in the country

Like Wrigley Field, Lincoln Park Zoo—the nation's largest free zoo—sits in the middle of a Chicago neighborhood. In this case, it's Lincoln Park, Chicago's upscale Yuppie neighborhood, which means that you can walk to just about everything from there—from deep dish pizzerias, to trendy shops and hair salons.

In fact, walking seems to be the operative word here. You can walk right up to the Zoo from nearby bus stops, parking lots, or neighborhoods. (For those who do drive, street parking is available if you circle the blocks a few times. Otherwise, lot parking is available for about $10.)

But you should take advantage of the walking. You can walk the length of the Zoo, enjoying the increasing greenness of it—Mayor Daley has been busy creating a greener Chicago. You can also walk to the Lincoln Park Conservatory (a hop, skip, and a jump from here), the Peggy Notebaert Nature Museum, and the Chicago Historical Society from the zoo. You can also take a museum/zoo break and let the kids play on the public playground across from the zoo on Cannon Drive.

Lincoln Park Zoo is clean, photogenic, and convenient — a sort of Disneyland zoo—complete with food courts that offer everything from Italian to Mexican to veggie burgers, an endangered species carousel, and paddleboat rides on the lagoon. Do you want to impress out-of-town guests? Take them here. It's the perfect backdrop to anything Chicago—you can see the blue of Lake Michigan and the city's skyline. (Is it a wonder the zoo has been featured in Hollywood films such as *Return to Me*?)

You also get a great cross-section of Chicagoans. One recent morning, the city's inhabitants were out walking, including an elderly couple that shouted "good morning," to a young dad carrying an infant to school kids on a field trip. And lots and lots of strollers. Of course, the animals aren't so bad, either.

A beautiful pond hosts ducks, geese, and trumpeter swans. You can see the Polar Bears and Lions pacing on their rocks, and the sea lions frolicking in their water homes. You can visit the Great Ape House, the Primate House, and the Lion House.

The zoo's well-known Pritzker's Children's Zoo, famous for its patient zookeepers and hands-on activities, is worth the trip alone. However, it's being renovated. It will open again in Spring 2005, with brand-new features, including a riverbed, caves, and woodlands with beavers, bears, and more.

In the meantime, check out the farm in the zoo—the closest many urban kids will get to farmland. Kids can watch a vegetable garden being planted, feed cows at the dairy barn, and visit the "general store"—a small house where the zoo volunteers carry out the day's activities, such as baking cookies, churning milk into butter, and story time. There's also the famous baby chick hatchery, where children get to watch new chicks emerging. They can also pet bunnies, snakes, and (eek!) rats in the main barn.

Another Lincoln Park Zoo plus is that you can rent paddleboats on its lagoon. Try it with older kids. You'll feel like you're leaving the city without going anywhere. The zoo also has special programs throughout the year, such as the Zoolights festival during December, a series of concerts throughout the year, Tiny Tykes story time for 3 to 4-year-olds, and Bedtime Buddies, animal bedtime stories for kids who show up in their animal-print pj's. (Parents should keep theirs at home.)

All the perks are great, of course, but the real lure of Lincoln Park Zoo is that it's always there, always free, and always available. It offers a perfect spur-of-the-moment, 'What Shall We Do Today?' excursion, even in winter. Just bundle up.

lillstreet art center

✣ *4401 N. Ravenswood, Chicago IL 60640*
773-769-4226
Ideal Age Group: 2 to 17
Admission: Varies, depending on class/event
www.lillstreet.com

art classes for budding picassos

Remember art classes as a kid? Elmer's glue, construction paper, and rounded-tip scissors? The Lillstreet Art Center takes kids' art classes to a whole new level. On the corner of Montrose and Ravenswood in the heart of Chicago's Ravenswood neighborhood (and right off the CTA Brown Line; some street parking available), the Lillstreet Art Center sits in a rehabbed former warehouse. It's now a 24,000-square-foot gallery with classrooms, state-of-the-art pottery and art equipment, and two rooms designed especially for children. The outside is painted in bright colors, and inside it's also warm and bright. After 28 years in Lincoln Park, Lillstreet Art Center seems to have found its home.

And what a home it is! The real draw of Lillstreet—the largest ceramic facility in the Midwest—is that they treat the children with as much respect as they treat the adults. Their mission is, in part, "to provide the best teaching for its students," and they seem to do just that. Barbara Kurtz, a working artist and Director of Administration, says, "I would have loved to come here as a kid."

Children's classes, which typically run about 10 weeks are limited to 8 to 12 children—so kids get lots of individual attention—and cost between $70 to $155. In the toddler classes, kids come with parents or caregivers, but as soon as your child turns 3 $\frac{1}{2}$, he or she can explore the art on his or her or her own (the parent must just attend the first class.) Toddler classes include Toddler Clay and Junior Jasper Johns (2-D mixed-media).

Slightly older kids can create their own cast of characters in Heroes and Villains (who knows, maybe your kid will be the next Stan Lee?), or they can hone their budding Gary Larson skills in Drawing and Cartoons. Young theater lovers can check out Curtain Call, where they'll create puppets, costumes, and scenery, and where they'll stage an end-of-the-class performance with their creations.

Teenagers can use nontraditional and recycled materials to create masterpieces in Exploring Found Materials, or they can learn how to create mosaics or sculpt figures. If they have a lot of teenage angst, sign them up for poetry and writing classes—or mask making, where they can create a new persona.

If you want some bonding time with your children, try side-by-side wheelthrowing, where you and your child can explore clay together, or some of the family programs, such as Architecture for Pets—create a castle for your goldfish! Or consider getting together with friends or family for a custom class—you choose the subject and material.

Lillstreet also comes through for summers and holidays—5- to 17- year-olds can take part in their art camps that offer everything from multimedia arts for the younger kids to metalsmithing and wheelthrowing for the older ones.

And the beauty of the place is that it's non-competitive, but serious. So it's perfect both for the dabbler and for youngsters who are trying to compile a portfolio for art school admission. Also, Lillstreet is a whole community of artists, with working artists—painters, sculptors, potters—renting studio space upstairs. (Go ahead and browse through their studios. You'll find wonderful vases, jewelry, dishes, mosaics that make great one-of-a-kind shower or wedding gifts.) If you want lunch or a snack, you can grab a bite in the Lillstreet Cafe, where they sell sandwiches, soups, coffee, and tea. But your better bet is to take a walk west on Montrose where you'll find everything from Thai to Chinese to Middle Eastern.

margie's candies

❈ *1960 N. Western Avenue, Chicago, IL 60647*

773-384-1035

Ideal Age Group: 4 to 16

Admission: Meals average $6 with dessert

a time capsule of old chicago (with awesome sundaes)

If you want an authentic Chicago experience—and you're a high-butterfat-rich-ice-cream-and/or-hand-dipped-candy buff, take the kids to Margie's Candies, a Northwest Side staple for more than 85 years. Margie's still stands on a rather dilapidated corner in Bucktown—now a mecca for Chicago's hipsters, but long a working-class neighborhood where residents shopped, and ate, within walking distance of their homes.

You'll know Margie's as soon as you see it, with its crowded storefront windows filled with dolls, seasonal decorations, and general tchotchkes. Inside, it's cramped as well. More blank-eyed dolls in silk dresses line the shelves, interspersed with stuffed animals. The front of the restaurant barely has room for the register and food prepping area, across from the candy counter. Walk a little bit to the back—you have to squeeze through the aisles—and take a seat at one of the small tan booths that encircle the room, each with a tabletop jukebox—two selections for a quarter. (Make sure you check out the Beatles, Al Capone, and Frank Sinatra memorabilia behind a glass case, remnants of past customers. More recent visitors have included Britney Spears, Michael Jordan, and many of the current Cubs.)

In short, much looks as it did about 85 years ago when Green immigrant Peter George Poulos opened this ice cream parlor on North Western Avenue, and named it after his daughter. It's still run by the Poulos family, specifically Margie's son Peter Poulos, a podiatrist whose grandfather made him a cradle in the back of the store. (Margie used to run the cash register until her death.)

Why does everyone come to Margie's Candies? Owner Poulos says it's for "the Margie's Experience," which means, in a nutshell, a snapshot of Chicago life that almost belongs in a museum. That, and pretty good ice cream—try the hot fudge sundae, or the five scoop tummy buster—and candy, everything from rock candy to chocolate mints to pecan, caramel, and chocolate Terrapins. All fresh. "The fudge eaten today is made today," says Poulos.

And it's really reasonable—just under $5 for the Jumbo Atomic Fudge Sundae, a huge three-scoop concoction with hot fudge, whipped cream, and sugar cookies. The rest of the menu consists of very plain food—not even guilty pleasures, just Americana, circa 1945—meatloaf, egg salad, chicken noodle soup, stuffed tomato, and a retro Hawaiian Plate. Our total bill, for two meals and one Atomic Fudge Sundae came to just over $14.

Margie's is perfect for small birthday parties, or an after-city-outing treat. It's like visiting your grandmother's or great aunt's parlor down to the aromas—a mixture of fudge and something suspiciously like mothballs.

In the end, Margie's Candies survives the Chicago way—with lots of hard work and heart. As you exit, check out a sign hanging by the cash register that promises a free ice cream cone to local students if they bring in a report card with an "A," or a free banana split to go if they can prove they brought a "C" up to an "A."

the mexican fine arts museum

❖ *1852 W. 19th St., Chicago, IL 60608*
312-738-1503
Ideal Age Group: 6 and up
Admission: Free
www.mfacmchicago.org

color, culture, and neighborhood

If you travel a mile or so west of the University of Illinois Chicago campus, you'll find yourself in Pilsen/Little Village—Chicago's vibrant Mexican-American neighborhood and the largest Mexican-American community in the Midwest.

It's a real Chicago neighborhood—still low on the trendy townhouses and coffee shops. Instead, you'll see Chicago cops eating in the restaurants on 18th Street, with their bikes and cars parked on the street. You'll find a host of little stores, everything from health food to health clinics to beauty salons, with signs in Spanish and English, and colorful murals on the building walls. In the summer, you can buy watermelons, mangoes, and tortillas from street vendors.

The jewel of this neighborhood is the Mexican Fine Arts Museum, which stands on 19th Street in a beautiful Art Deco building with convenient parking right on the street. Inside you'll find traditional and contemporary Mexican and Mexican-American drawings, paintings, prints, papier-mâché, ceramics, fabrics, murals, and photographs, all manner of things for kids and adults to delight in.

The vibrant history of Mexico comes alive in this one-story art enclave (confession here: It's one of my favorite Chicago art museums). The museum provides a wonderful opportunity to teach children about art and culture. Every exhibition is bilingual, so brush up on your Spanish before coming, or ask children learning Spanish to help you translate.

The museum, which charges no admission, has an extensive permanent collection—more than 3,500 pieces, including works by Diego Rivera, devotional paintings and carved saints, and vintage United Farm Workers Union posters—plus special temporary exhibitions, such as a Frida Kahlo show that ran several years ago. An annual highlight (starting in September) is the country's largest Dia de Muertos (Day of the Dead) exhibition, where local community members help construct an altar to honor their dead.

Kids will love the humor, color, and liveliness, such as the wall display devoted to the Virgin of Guadalupe, including the *VG Gets Her Green Card* and the *Mona Luna*. For history buffs, there's a gallery dedicated to Mexican independence, with features on the Spanish invasion of Mexico in the fifteenth century, with masks, murals, paintings, and textiles. (Don't miss the devil costume with mask, which reflects the missionaries' impact on the indigenous cultures.)

To learn more about Mexican history, visit the Interactive Resource Center, where, in a room full of Macs—not all working, like at any computer lab—kids can learn about the last Aztec emperor, traditional Mexican instruments, or women in ancient Mexico. (Note for parents of young girls: The museum seems to take special care in presenting a positive role of women in history.)

In the textile gallery, you can learn about clothing from different regions—why they wore what they did. Above the different textiles you'll find questions to provoke discussion, such as "Can you identify which elements of design or decoration were influenced by European fashion?" It also features an exhibition on traditional dyes—derived from coffee beans, walnuts, and pomegranates.

For young artists, the museum hosts family days on appointed Sundays. Children ages 6 to 12 can participate in hands-on art projects. They also offer free summer art classes for 5- to 13-year-olds. In the spring, don't miss the special Dia Del Nino (Day of the Child) festival, where kids can participate in art activities. The museum also has a Performing Arts Department, with two annual festivals centered around concerts, dances, films, and theater productions.

Like most museums these days, the Mexican Fine Arts Museum has a store—but this one is worth a special mention. The Tienda Tzintzuntzan gift shop offers real treasures for kids and adults, including beautifully constructed jewelry, vases, mirrors, and paintings for grown-ups or teens, and Mexican toys, games, books, and Day of the Dead figurines for little ones.

Also, take a look at the skyline from here—especially if you visit the museum on a winter's day in late afternoon. It's as lovely as it gets—the buildings twinkling against the winter's deep sky. And at any time of the year, stroll down 18th Street and visit one of the small restaurants such as Tacos Don Chon at 1743 W. 18th Street or Carnitas Uruapan at 1725 W. 18th Street. You're also close enough to Taylor Street (Chicago's Little Italy) to make the short trip for some excellent Italian beef, pizza, or gelato.

morton arboretum

※ *4100 Illinois Route 53, Lisle, IL 60532-1293*
630-968-0074
Ideal Age Group: 2 to 18
Admission: Adults $5; seniors $4; children $2;
children under 2, free
www.mortonarb.org

a touch of wisconsin in illinois

If you'd like to get away to wide, open spaces and don't have the time to drive up I-94 to Wisconsin, try going a little west instead—to Lisle and its Morton Arboretum, 25 miles west of downtown Chicago. You'll find an amazing 1,700 acres of land that takes you far from the urban landscape.

What is the Arboretum? Simply a celebration of nature—in the form of beautiful gardens, plant collections, and natural spaces. Founded in 1922 by Joy Morton of Morton Salt fame, its mission is simple: to conserve trees and other plants for a healthier world. (It's also one of the largest nature research programs in the nation. They collect plants for the National Cancer Institute, for example.)

There are not a lot of frills here—just nature at her best. It's open 365 days a year, from 7 a.m. to approximately sunset. They have more than 350 classes, seminars, and programs, and miles of hiking trails (you can just go and be in nature, or read all the accompanying signs for an education), and even 9 miles of paved roads for those who like to do their sightseeing from inside a car. (When it's 45 degrees or warmer outside, they offer 50-minute guided tours upon the Acorn Express, an open-air train.)

You can put on your hiking shoes and get lost in nature. They frown on picking flowers and plant samples, but encourage leaf collecting. They'll even give kids a leaf-collecting bag at Visitor's Services.

Other kid-friendly activities include the seasonal festivities—they offer the Fall Color Festival, with a corn maze and book fair (and hand-dipped taffy apples, too!). Or in the spring you might consider visiting for the Arboretum After Dark, where you get to walk through the woods at night, listening to the sounds and learning about the habitats of the nocturnal animals who live there.

In the winter, kids 5 and older can rent snowshoes to track through the winter wonderlands and see the leafless beauty of the trees. And there is beauty year-round! (They've even set up a Bloom 'n' Color hotline at 630-719-7955 so you can find out what's in color in any given week.)

If you'd like more structured time at the Arboretum, sign your kids up for classes such as Wild Places, where 2- and 3-year-olds find their own special place in the woods, and hunt for frogs and other critters. They also may like Wiggly Squiggly Worms, where 4- and 5-year-olds find out everything they've always wanted to know about worms but were afraid to ask.

Budding bird watchers, aged 8 to 10, can join Breakfast with the Birds, a bird-walking tour, with breakfast, in which they also study bird artifacts (such as feathers) under a microscope. Or the whole family can take part in the Family Fireside, where you'll sing campfire songs, tell stories, and go on a night hike.

Currently, the Arboretum is in the process of a 43-million-dollar renovation, including building the largest children's garden in the Chicago area—four acres of gardens with a field station for classes and outdoor exhibits. It's slated to be finished mid-2005. Until then, the whole thing is a children's garden.

the museum of science and industry

✳ *57th Street and Lake Shore Drive,*
Chicago, IL 60637
773-684-1414
Ideal Age Group: 5 to 17
Admission: Adults $9; 3 to 11 year-olds $5; seniors $7.50
Discounts for Chicago residents. Check out their free days.
Parking $8 per vehicle.
www.msichicago.org

computers, coal mines, and cadavers

This majestic building—across the street from Lake Michigan in Hyde Park—has been in Chicago in one form or another since the first World's Fair in 1893 when it was the Palace of Fine Arts. In the 1930s, a Sears Roebuck & Company executive restored the building to mimic an "industrial enlightenment" museum he had visited in Munich, where the focus was interactive exhibits. Today, more than two million visitors enter the doors each year. And interaction is still the name of the game.

As a kid, I thought this was just the coolest thing—and it still is. You could test your ability to discern musical tones (I was tone deaf), visit an old-fashioned town, get your picture taken in an antique car, and see a human body cut into slices—sanitized and nearly unrecognizable behind plates of glass so the gore factor was low—but still. . . .

Today, it's more high-tech, and consumer savvy (check out the lower level; you'll feel as though you've walked into Woodfield Mall by mistake). However, it's still quirky, interactive, and captivating—especially for the young thinkers, inventors, and science buffs in your life. And many of its old stars still stand.

You can still see the cut-up bodies. You can still explore a WWII captured German submarine—or travel down a working coalmine shaft from 1933 to become a miner for an hour. (Non-claustrophobes only!) Planes, trains, and automobile buffs will delight in a 3,000-foot model railroad, or walking through a Boeing 727, Apollo 8 Spacecraft, Lunar Module Trainer, or the 1914 Model T.

More imaginative children may take to the exquisite Fairy Castle. Colleen Moore, a 1920s silent-movie actress who furnished this room-size doll house with the help of an architect, interior designer, and Beverly Hills jeweler (apparently, she needed something to occupy her time once the talkies came in to vogue).

You can still see baby chicks hatch, and The Hall of Communications still exists, just in a new incarnation. It's now NetWorld—a computer will take your picture and flash it on a large screen television, you can watch newscasts from around the world, and you can still check out the whispering chamber, an acoustically perfect room. (You whisper to your partner 50 feet behind you and when he replies, he sounds as though he's two inches from your ear.)

If you're with young children, make sure you head to a more recent addition, the Idea Factory. Located in the basement, it's where young kids—through interactive play—learn the fundamentals of construction, light, and color—they can even construct and navigate their own boats. The museum also offers special programs, such as Snoozeums, where kids 7 to 14 can stay overnight at the museum, and A Taste of Science, a one-day workshop for 1st through 6th graders and their parents/caregivers.

This museum has so many goodies, it's possible to feel overwhelmed by all the tempting choices, and some may not even be exhibits. (When we walked in recently, a young

woman greeted us with what looked like an ice cream cart—
she asked us if we'd like to make some slime.)

The best way, we decided, was to approach the museum
like a buffet. You have a host of entries from which to choose.

Pick a few favorites each time, and save the rest for another
trip. Of course, this large selection bodes well for families or
groups who have a range of different interests. You can each
go your own way, and meet up again later.

naper settlement

523 S. Webster Street, Naperville, IL 60540

630-420-6010

Ideal Age Group: 1st through 8th grade

Admission: Adults $6.50; seniors $5.50; children $4

www.napersettlement.com

a walk into the past

Would you like to take your kids back in time so that they can experience the lives of the first settlers in the Midwest, and see the houses in which these pioneers lived, and the buildings in which they worked and worshipped? Trek out west to Naperville—a good 45 miles from the Loop—to visit Naper Settlement, a living museum with shops, houses, and civic buildings peopled with costumed actors who go about their day-to-day lives while greeting the visitors.

Naper Settlement sits nonchalantly near downtown Naperville, an upscale western suburb known for its famous Riverwalk. The settlement—really a whole campus of authentic and authentically recreated buildings—illustrates a Midwestern agrarian settlement from the 19th century, most of it based on Naperville's actual history.

We went in the middle of winter—when the campus and main building are open, but the historic buildings are not. Unlike in warmer weather, there were no costumed interpreters to guide us. Instead we had the option of renting an audio tour or just simply strolling the grounds, which are lovely at any time of year—peaceful and a world away.

The grounds include a blacksmith shop, print shop, stonecarver's shop, and firehouse, with a hand-pumper within. You'll also get to check out a post office with an 1840s interior, and a log house, similar to Naperville's first homes. Kids might enjoy visiting a schoolhouse—an original building that once stood in southern Naperville, with actual graffiti carved by the 19th-century schoolchildren still on the wall.

There's also a mini historical society in the main building—with a distinctly European bent. (You may want to read up on Native American history before or after to get a full perspective on Midwest settlements.)

Naper Settlement also offers a host of classes, programs, and events for kids. Past events have included a one-man show on Thomas Edison; Christmas Memories, where you can take a horse-drawn carriage ride, kids can get their faces painted, and you can meet up with Father Christmas (Santa Claus, circa 1850s). The festivities come complete with pioneer carolers.

In the summer, children can attend Camp Naper. You can host birthday parties here, or sleepovers. You can even have your kids take Manners for Minors, where they learn old-fashioned civility—but you may want to skip some of that and just let them have fun.

There's ample free parking, and restrooms with diaper-changing stations. If you'd like to take a break for lunch, take a quick walk across the street and you'll be in Naperville's Riverwalk, a 2-plus-mile park along the DuPage River lined with plenty of restaurants and stores.

north park village nature center

❋ *5801 N. Pulaski Road, Chicago, IL 60646*
312-744-5472
Ideal Age Group: Stroller to 14
Admission: Free
www.cityofchicago.org/Environment/Natural
Resources/NorthParkVillage.html

take a walk on the wild side

I found out about the North Park Village Nature Center the way most Chicagoans do—through word of mouth. It's a sort of secret hideaway for the city's nature buffs who don't want to venture far to see natural ecosystems. Located on the city's northwest side, near Pulaski and Peterson, it's easy to get to and hard to leave.

You can get there via public transportation—the Pulaski bus stops right in front of the center's entrance. Or you can drive. It's just minutes from Eden's Expressway and parking's free and ample. (Of course, bike riding may be the best way to start your nature trek.) When you get there, be prepared for beauty. When I visited recently on a rainy fall day, a deer quietly munched on some leaves at the start of the walking trail. No one else was around, save one photographer trying to get some shots in before the sun set.

Run under the auspices of the Chicago Department of Environment, North Park is the city's only bona fide nature center, whose mission reads, in part "to provide urban citizens with an opportunity to interact with wildlife, plants, and other natural resources." They accomplish this by maintaining Illinois' original four ecosystems within the 46 preserved acres, and providing educational classes and programs for both children and adults. (The volunteers at the center have replanted hundreds of indigenous trees, wildflowers, and shrubs since the city took over the land in 1992.)

The city built the center on the lands of an old farm and landscape nursery, which for a time became the city's Municipal Tuberculosis Sanitarium (which explains the heavy brick, nearly prison-like buildings that dot the surrounding land). Today, one of these buildings serves as a nursing home and another is a large gym.

The center is open from 10 a.m. to 4 p.m., unless they're hosting a special event.

Visit the Interpretive Center first—a small cabin near the walking trail and organic garden—which contains educational resources, helpful staff, and some small, local animals such as turtles, snakes, and salamanders. The educational facility provides hands-on instruction for kids in recycling, composing, tree planting, and gardening, among other things.

Then choose one of the two walking loops—the main one is a half-mile, the larger one goes around this one—and save the other one for another day. These stroller-friendly trails allow kids to observe savannahs, wetlands, woodlands, and prairie, and their natural denizen—everything from red-winged blackbirds to foxes to ducks, geese, and turtles. You'll find helpful signs along the way. However, let your eyes and ears be your primary guides. (See how many different bird calls you can hear; see how many varieties of flowers.)

The Nature Center is committed to education and offers a host of special programs. For example, 5- to 14-year-olds can become EcoExplorers at the center's annual summer camp. You can also sign children up for the Prairie Prowls and Wetlands Walks, tours designed especially for young ones.

Each month the center presents special seasonal features, such as the Maple Syrup Festival in March, where kids can learn how to tap maple trees and taste the final product on pancakes, the scarecrow building contest in October, or the winter solstice in December, where storytelling around a bonfire is capped by a walk through a luminary-lit trail.

You don't have to go far to enjoy nature. You just have to know how to get there.

the old town school of folk music

※ *4544 N. Lincoln Avenue, Chicago, IL 60625*
773-728-6000
Ideal Age Group: Infant to 18
Admission: Varies, depending on class/event
www.oldtownschool.org

for young music hipsters

If you want the hippest place around to take kids to learn all the great stuff about music, movement, and art, take them to the Old Town School of Folk Music, a Chicago mainstay—it's where Chicago musicians take their own kids, and the training and performing ground for many Chicago music legends, including John Prine, Mahalia Jackson, and Steve Goodman.

Even though the school has changed locations several times since its advent in 1957, it's still filled with the same spirit—of quality, heartfelt music taught by some of the best instructors in the country.

The school began on North Avenue in Old Town (hence the name), and moved to Armitage in 1968, now a branch called the Old Town School Children's Center. However, since 1998, the home base—for adults and children—is a 43,000-square-foot Lincoln Square location, right in the heart of one of the most vibrant neighborhoods the city has to offer. Inside, on any day of the week, you'll find a variety of music lovers of all ages jamming, strumming guitars, or just hanging out in the small lobbies or café.

One of the big draws for kids at the Old Town School is Wiggleworms, classes for 6-month- to 3-year-olds, in which kids and parents sing, play rhythm instruments, play finger games, and take part in circle dances. These classes are so popular, they now have Wigglegrads, for 3- to 4-year-olds, and bilingual Wiggleworms (you can sing in Spanish, French, or German). They also offer these classes at various locations around Chicago, including Evanston, Hyde Park, and Hinsdale.

Kids can also take a variety of music, art, and dance and theater classes, including Irish Fiddle (learn jigs and reel!), Big and Little Drummers, and their bilingual Spanish-English children's choir. Or you can sign up for private lessons, on instruments ranging from banjo to cello to fiddle to bass guitar.

You can also sign 5- to 10-year-olds up for various summer camps, which include guitar, drumming, dancing writing, filmmaking, and improvisational theater. Camp runs Monday through Friday, from 9 to 4.

One of the great treats about the new Lincoln Square location is the chance to explore the neighborhood. Before or after class, make sure you stroll down Lincoln Avenue and check out Delicatessen Meyer at 4750 N. Lincoln for great pickles, rye bread, and sandwiches, or the magical Merz Apothecary, at 4716 N. Lincoln, a traditional German pharmacy with herbal remedies, treats, and body care.

the peace school

❊ *3121 N. Lincoln Avenue, Chicago, IL 60657*

Phone: 773-248-7959

Ideal Age Group: 4 and up

Admission: Per class/series

www.peaceschool.org

meditate on peace while learning tai kwon do

On a bustling stretch of Lincoln Avenue north of Lincoln Park among the mom-and-pop restaurants and specialty stores, sits a beautiful old Chicago building with a large second-floor window. It used to be a shoe store, and the wares were placed in this large display area. Instead of shoes, they now peddle peace.

This is the home of the Peace School—a nonprofit organization that was founded by MyungSu Y.S. Kim, a Korean immigrant, and founder of the first Peace Day celebration, now an international event. (MyungSu Kim has since died. His son, Charles now runs the school.) Inside, kids of all ages can join grown-ups in peaceful martial arts and yoga classes. Children as young as four are welcome.

Each class is conducted on the theme of peace and include Peace Exercise Yoga, Peace Relaxation, a martial arts form based on Tai Kwon Do, and some breathing meditation (known as—what else?—Peace Breathing). The classes teach motor and balance skills, as well as increase self-confidence. They're also fun. Children can take classes with parents, and there's little pressure to conform or perform. Each class ends with a prayer for world peace, and for a designated country of the day. So kids learn geography as well as serenity.

Basically, volunteers run the Peace School, so don't expect any polished marketing efforts or rigid scheduling. In fact, they cheerfully admit that the schedule can be confusing and fluid. Generally, you'll pay about $40 a month for classes, with slight discounts for members.

In conjunction with the Mayor's Office of Special Events, the Peace School still spearheads Chicago's Peace Day celebration, which is held at different locations each year. Last year, it returned home to the Peace School, where a host of adults and children from around the city danced—everything from belly dancing to African dance—and sang. It was a festive occasion, with an after-performance smorgasbord of food donated by local restaurants. This is the spirit of the school and it's a good one.

peggy notebaert nature museum

❋ *2430 North Cannon Drive, Chicago, IL 60614*
773-755-5100
Ideal Age Group: 3 to 12
Admission: Adults $7; seniors and students 13–22 $5;
kids 3–12 $4. Discounts for Chicago residents.
www.naturemuseum.org

a hands-on lesson in conservation

This modern monolith at Cannon Drive and Fullerton Avenue, a stone's throw from Lincoln Park Zoo and the Conservatory, is actually a reincarnation of Chicago's first museum, the Chicago Academy of Sciences, an amazing nature museum that used to reside quietly on North Clark Street.

In 1999, it became the Peggy Notebaert Nature Museum—with money from a local donor, Ms. Notebaert's husband. Now it's an extravaganza of sorts—big, bold, and slick. (But still green. They use solar heating and recycled materials.)

Surrounding the museum are prairie gardens. Inside is a celebration of Chicago's animals, insects, plants, and ecosystems. You'll learn all about this through presentations, movies, and interactive exhibits at this museum. For example, left over from the original Clark Street location is the Wilderness Walk, which invites you to stroll through Chicago's landscape before it was Chicago. This includes dunes, the savannah, and the prairie—small exhibits that you can walk through that recreate the lands before the John Hancock and Sears Tower were built with replicated animals and plants.

Also, make sure to check out the Butterfly Haven. It's a magical mystery tour of butterflies—about 1,000 of them—in all the hues of the rainbow, flying around a large room, with some transforming before your eyes as they emerge from their chrysalises. "You're in the Caribbean here," said the volunteer, referring to the waterfall, humidity, and sun-drenched windows. (Our advice? Dress lightly. Layer!) The sign at the exit says "Check yourself for passengers before you leave," and that's the beauty of it—these butterflies are completely free, and the kids love it. As you exit, check out the interactive display on metamorphosis.

Young tots may enjoy the Hands-On Habitat, and budding greens can check out the Extreme Green House, complete with a hands-on display on alternative energy. They also have a wonderful water lab, where school kids gleefully create rivers and dams in the "stream table," with water and sand everywhere, including on the floor, chairs, and the kids themselves. You also have an opportunity to make the Chicago River flow backward (and learn why it actually does).

The museum also hosts temporary exhibits, each lasting three to four months. Recent exhibits include one on naturalist Jane Goodall, another on crocodiles, and one on Monster Creepy Crawlies. Also, check out their kids' programs, including the Knee-High Naturalists, where 4- and 5-year-olds visit neighborhood trees, grow their own, and sample "treets."

They also offer nature camps for kids ages 5 to 14. Depending on the age, kids learn about photosynthesis, get to explore a real prairie, and even go camping. I miss the old, cozy Academy of Sciences, but you can't argue with success—not when it teaches kids the beauty and value of preserving our natural lands in an age that increasingly dismisses it.

piven theatre workshop

✻ *927 Noyes Street, Evanston, IL 60201*

847-866-6597

Ideal Age Group: 4th grade through high school

Admission: Approximately $350 for 14-week classes

www.piventheatre.org

theater improvisation for confidence and culture

If you're a Chicago theater buff, you'll have heard of the Piven Theatre Workshop, founded by actors Joyce and Byrne Piven. It's been the training ground for many of Chicago's most gifted stage and screen performers, including Joan and John Cusack, Aidan Quinn, Rosanna Arquette, Lili Taylor, and, of course, Piven progeny, Jeremy Piven.

What's so great about Piven? It's that they've stayed true to their roots—improvisational theater with its original intent, which is not so much about comedy as it is being comfortable and natural on stage. The classes—which range from those for 4th graders to adults—draw everyone from wallflowers to professional actors, and it's a pretty level playing field.

These classes are held near Northwestern's campus in the Noyes Street Cultural Center in Evanston, a big community center. (It's near the El and there's also ample lot parking). There are not a lot of frills here—just hard-working and dedicated teachers, and the starkest of rooms become magical under their nurturing care.

In fact, the emphasis in the classes is not on turning out stars, but rather turning out happier, more creative, and confident souls. Kids can start with classes such as Theatre Games and Story Theatre—which is all about listening and trusting rather than memorizing or performing. (Kids will play everything from Red Light, Green Light to Freeze Tag—all with a theatrical bent.)

By the time they're in junior high, kids can take Improvisation and Scene Study and Advanced Story Theatre—even Stage Combat! High schoolers can take such advanced classes as Commedia and Performance, based on a highly stylized late Italian Renaissance theater form, where they design their own costumes and stage props. They can also try out for Young People's Company, where they get to perform for the public. (The Piven Theatre also has a Resident Theatre Ensemble that performs everything from Shakespeare to Mamet, as well as original works.)

Kids come from all over the Chicago area to study at Piven—from Racine, Wisconsin, and Moline, Illinois. If you'd like to check it out before you sign your child up, come on the last day of classes, when they welcome the public to observe.

As long as you make the trek to Evanston, also check out the Actors Gymnasium, the Circus & Performing Arts School (847-328-2795), also housed in the Noyes Cultural Arts Center. Kids can learn to juggle, walk on stilts, and tumble. (They even have parent-tot dance and gymnastics classes.)

the puppet parlor theatre

✳ *1922 W. Montrose, Chicago, IL 60613*
773-774-2919
Ideal Age Group: 5 to 10
Admission: $10

gothic thrills for young theater buffs

In a charming storefront theater on West Montrose—down the street from a Starbucks and other modern conveniences—is the National Marionette Theatre of Chicago, a grand name for a small treasure. This elegant, quirky puppet theater hosts a variety of shows for children and adults, mostly fairy and folktales. The theater itself seems to belong to a fairy tale, as though you could turn around and it would be gone, or that it appears only once in a blue moon, like "Brigadoon."

In the front window sit real-as-life handmade puppets. Inside the cozy, two-room building you'll find a cramped box office with a sign saying "Please don't smoke. The puppets don't like it," and in the back, a small theater with folding chairs and a hand-constructed stage. They've wrapped cotton around the stage lights, so they look like clouds—a sort of Music Box Theater for kids. The walls are painted a deep burgundy, accented with candelabras and baroque paintings.

Owner and founder Ralph Kipniss, a former ballet dancer with Ruth Page, has been running this puppet theater for thirty years. He does the whole thing with his partner and a few protégés. There are usually four of them standing above the small stage, working the lights and manipulating the stunning puppets that, when you first see gliding across the stage, take your breath away.

At the Puppet Parlor they perform classic fairy tales, folktales, and annotated operas and classics, such as the *Magic*

Flute and *A Midsummer Night's Dream*. Ralph and company carve, paint, and dress all the puppets themselves in a basement workshop jammed to the gills with puppets in waiting. They re-create everyone from Mae West to the Tin Man, works of art produced on a Singer sewing machine and a woodcarving table.

These puppets stroll, dance, and sing during the telling of the stories and they soon become real to the audience. In *Hansel and Gretel*—an operetta—the young audience sits mesmerized watching this spectacle, much different than the current crop of Disney movies and music videos.

This is not slick theatre—it has big heart. Kipniss tapes the actors' voices ahead of time—there's not enough room in the small theatre to have live performers backstage—and the taped voices accompany the deft puppeteers. It's quirky and full of fun—you can hear the puppeteers talking to one another at times—and during *Hansel and Gretel* they lost sound for a moment. The humanness of the production complements the lifelike puppets. They even serve popcorn and punch at the intermission.

As an added bonus, the Puppet Parlor offers puppet-making classes to kids and adults. Kids 10 years and older can learn to make puppets, starting with hand ones, and move to the more complex. Also, the Puppet Parlor offers birthday parties for $12 a child for groups of 12 or more—kids can see a performance and even get a short lesson in puppeteering. (You'd be hard pressed to find a more interesting birthday party venue in Chicago.)

redmoon theatre outdoor pageants/festivals

❊ *Festivals held around the city. Theater located at 1438 W. Kinzie Street, Chicago, IL 60622*

312-850-8440

Ideal Age Group: 4 to 18

Admission: Outdoor pageants, free. Other programs vary.

www.redmoon.org

giant puppets! minstrels! audience participation! if kids ruled the theater world

I first witnessed a Redmoon Theatre event at their now-defunct, but previously annual All Hallow's Eve parade, held in Logan Square. In this wonderful extravaganza, the actors of Redmoon dressed up in giant masks, with puppets, live musicians and other effects. These actors led the community—hundreds of adults, kids, and teens—some dressed up, others not—winding through the city streets in a very calm bacchanalia. It was a sort of sober Mardi Gras—the whimsy and artistry without the booze and lasciviousness. It was a magical celebration of a cultural rite.

Once this pageant grew too large and unwieldy—and expensive—Redmoon decided to focus their energies on their Winter Pageant—now held at their new theater space in West Town, where up to 500 people participate in this community-based celebration of the solstice and the changing of the seasons. This is a perfect opportunity for creative kids to be in a show. They can participate in the pageant itself if they like—performing alongside professional Chicago actors—or they can do the pre-pageant work by joining

Redmoon's Shrine workshops in October and November where adults and kids build shrines in honor of recently deceased loved ones, to be used in the December pageant.

Redmoon—which also performs literary theater at their home office—have not forsaken their outdoor spectacle roots. In fact, they've simply created a new one—84 Nights—to take the place of All Hallow's Eve. It will debut September 2004, and will feature masks, puppets, and live music. Since the theme will be Water and Work, they'll hold it near some Chicago body of water and create a circus atmosphere (more Cirque du Soleil than Ringling Bros.) where you can stand, sit, or walk around to view the different performances.

Redmoon embodies the best of Chicago theater, from Victory Gardens to Steppenwolf, with its energy, inclusiveness, and devotion to craft and community. It embodies perhaps better than any other theater in Chicago the European tradition of ritual and rites of passage. If you close your eyes a little, you could be on a hillside in Northern Europe in the seventeenth century, celebrating St. John's Eve with bonfires and drink.

the shedd aquarium

❊ *1200 S. Lake Shore Drive, Chicago IL 60605*

312-939-2435

Ideal Age Group: 4 to 17

Admission (original aquarium only): Adults $8; Children and seniors $6. More for special exhibits.

www.sheddaquarium.org

all the fish in the sea

What's not to like about the Shedd Aquarium? This monolithic structure right on the edge of Lake Michigan truly gives a feeling of ocean expanse to our inland sea. (It's also part of the three-part Chicago Museum Campus, which also includes the Field Museum and the Adler Planetarium.)

Now the Shedd is known for its multimillion-dollar Oceanarium and Wild Reef (which cost extra to get into), but since 1930, Chicago kids have loved (and still do) the low-rent original exhibits—tons of colorful fish from Asia, Africa, Australia, and Lake Michigan, swimming through numerous tanks throughout. This may be enough for one trip.

You may want to make a separate trip to check out the Caribbean Reef, home to 250 tropical reef animals, including sharks, eels, sea turtles, and a host of colorful fish. Or the Wild Reef, a 400,000-gallon shark habitat, where 25 sharks, including Japanese wobbegongs, zebras, and whitetip reef sharks swim in a replica of a reef ecosystem from the Philippines. It's located 25 feet below sea level, and these beautiful sharks share the water with barracudas and other reef predators.

Of course, the pièce de résistance is the Oceanarium, which opened in 1991. This 45-million-dollar, four-level venture is built on 1.8 acres of landfill. Its 215 windows offer a sweeping vista of Lake Michigan, and set the daily dolphin shows against the backdrop of the lake. The Oceanarium is a recreation of the Pacific northwest—the coast that runs from Oregon to Canada, with Beluga whales (which eat 40 to 80 pounds of food a day), Pacific white side dolphins, and harbor seals.

Each day you can watch these dolphins and whales dive and tailwalk (but reserve your seats early—it's first come, first serve). You can also take in the daily Caribbean Reef dive, where divers hand-feed the animals and describe the underwater goings-on with specially designed underwater microphones. The Aquarium also offers Habitat Chats, which, as the name implies, is an on-site educational discussion about the natural habitats of the museum's animals.

The museum offers special family programming throughout the year, such as Tots on Tuesday, with storytelling, crafts, videos, and singing and dancing for 3- to 5-year-olds. You can also sign up for Summer Camps, where kids can take classes such as Water Music I (learning about the "music" found in nature, such as animal songs), and Spineless Sea Sensations (jellyfish, anyone?), or Breakfast with the Animals (a look at what happens in the Aquarium each day before it opens to the public).

Since this is a highly popular museum, smart parents try to avoid crowds by coming early—early Sunday morning is especially good. The average visit takes about 2-and-a-half hours, so be prepared with snacks and other distractions. (They have a food court and more upscale restaurant, but also places to picnic.)

They have a small designated nursing area on the lower level, although nursing moms have found the small quiet nooks through the museum perfect for this activity. Another tip: The museum has designated free days, but unless you can tolerate crowds, word on the street is pay the extra money and enjoy the space.

short shakespeare! chicago shakespeare theater

✳ *800 E. Grand Avenue (Navy Pier),*
Chicago, IL 60611
312-595-5600
Ideal Age Group: 4th grade through high school
Admission: Varies, usually around $10 for children; adults, $15
www.chicagoshakes.com

brush up your shakespeare

In the middle of the carnival atmosphere of Navy Pier sits an amazingly beautiful theater—modeled after the Swan Theatre in Stratford, England. Wooden walls, beautiful padded seats, three-levels, including two balcony sections, and catwalks surround the stage.

In this space, magic happens. It rains, people fly through the air, and stories come to life before your eyes. This is the Chicago Shakespeare Theater, and now it's available for kids, too. This lovely 500-plus-seat in-the-round theater allows kids to see some of the best actors in Chicago speaking some of the finest written words in the English language for only $10 a pop—a fraction of the cost of the *Lion King*, for example.

Short Shakespeare! is an off-shoot of the enormously successful Chicago Shakespeare Theater, Chicago's only professional theater dedicated to Shakespeare's works, which gave its first performance on the roof of the Red Lion Pub in Lincoln Park nearly 15 years ago. In 1999, they moved into this seven-story $24 million Navy Pier venue. Short Shakespeare! uses the same actors and directors as the full-length shows—they just abridge the text so that running time is 75 minutes, and jazz the settings up a bit for accessibility. It starts during the school year, usually in April and May. Recent productions include *A Midsummer Night's Dream* and *Romeo and Juliet*.

They also run Short Shakespeare! during the summer, as part of the theater's LaSalle Bank Family Festival of Plays. During this time, they also feature a family musical, such as *Joseph and the Amazing Technicolor Dreamcoat, The Wizard of Oz,* or *The Little Mermaid* (not the Disney score!). They've even hosted a Second City event appropriate for families, *Hamlet: The Musical.*

The Short Shakespeare! performances are always followed by a 15-minute discussion led by the actors and a theater educator. And, don't worry, these performances are not just for kids. Adults who've shied away from Shakespeare will find great pleasure in these pieces. And even though the targeted audience is 4th graders through high schoolers, on any given day you'll find a line of strollers parked in the lobby. After all, you can never be too young to enjoy Shakespeare!

Another bonus is that the large theater allows for many walk-up possibilities. So you can make your way to Navy Pier, enjoy yourself walking around, and if you feel like it, simply walk up to the box office for tickets. (During the school year, there are matinees. During the summer, plays run on Thursday, Friday, and Saturday nights, with a Sunday matinee.)

south shore cultural center

❊ *7059 S. Lake Shore Drive, Chicago, IL 60649*
312-747-2536
Ideal Age Group: Toddler to high school
Admission: Varies, depending on class/event
www.chicagoparkdistrict.com

the gem of the south side

Drive along South Lake Shore Drive and you'll hit this beautiful Art Deco building (called the "Gem of the South Side"), located on a beautiful stretch of Lake Michigan—it sits on 60 acres of land. While the classes and events inside are some of the best the Chicago Park District has to offer, part of the lure of this place is simply the building itself. Your children will get to see majestic Chicago in all its glory.

The building has terra-cotta towers, a grand ballroom (which can be rented for weddings and other special events), and a stunning solarium. In the summer, you can take in concerts outside or in. The Paul Robeson Theater offers a theater series from March through May, local artists display their collections in the gallery, and classes are offered in everything from media arts, music, and dance. The Center puts on half-yearly special events, such as Kwanzaa celebrations, and African-American and Hispanic Heritage Months celebrations. (And, if you're lucky, you may get to see the magnificent horses that the Chicago Police Department keeps in the Cultural Center's stables. The building was originally constructed as the clubhouse of the South Shore Country Club, which was a big equestrian center.)

Begun as a country club for the weathy industrialists who lived in the South Shore neighborhood, the property, which is on the National Register of Historic Places, became the Cultural Center in 1984. When the Park District bought the building and the lands, they were going to tear it down, but community members demanded that they keep it standing (part of their intent was to gain access to a building that often had excluded others).

Today, in addition to the cultural center, it's a nature preserve, with a nine-hole golf course—right on the lake. Kids get their very own putting green, where they can take golf lessons. They've recently converted a dumping ground into a nature preserve with dunes, a boardwalk, and small pond.

The surrounding beach is also a good reason to make the trip—it's large, clean, and swimmable. You can also have glorious summer picnics in the adjoining park. If you want to see more of the South Shore, drive a mile north on South Lake Shore Drive to the the rehabilitated 63rd Street beach house, which now includes a serenity garden and a sprinkler park for kids.

trailside museum

❧ 738 Thatcher Avenue, River Forest, IL 60305

708-366-6530

Ideal Age Group: 4 to 12

Admission: Free

www.fpdcc.com

where chicago animals get rehabbed

Young nature buffs will love the Trailside Nature Museum, located at the corner of Thatcher and Chicago Avenues in River Forest—about nine miles from the Loop. This stately Victorian House, which was once a finishing school for wealthy young women, is now a halfway house for injured and abandoned local animals, who then serve as part of the nature museum (as a way to earn their keep, we suppose).

In 1917, the Cook County Forest Preserve District purchased the building and the surrounding land for use as their general headquarters. Finally, in 1931, they converted it to the Trailside Museum, whose official tagline is "Cook County's wildlife rehabilitation center for orphaned and injured native animals."

The attraction of this place is threefold: One, the price. It's free, and accessible. The Museum is open year-round, except for major holidays and Thursdays, and you can park on the street.

Second, the animals. Here, inside and out, you can see some of the area insects and animals—they are either brought in by local residents or found by the Park District. They are kept at the Trailside Museum until they can be returned to the wild, although some are lifers. It's an excellent opportunity for children to learn about their animal neighbors and the risks they face living in an urban setting.

Current residents include a one-eyed owl—he looked like a pirate perched in his 15-foot cage—vultures, raccoons, and a coyote that someone thought was an abandoned puppy. (Now, because he was taken from his mother too soon, he will remain at the museum for life.) They even rehabilitate squirrels and seagulls. At any given time, they keep around 40 animals here, all indigenous to Cook County. Inside the small two-room museum (it only takes about 15 minutes to go through this), they feature stuffed dead animals, animal skulls, and local injured birds—robins, crows, finches—plus some turtles and snakes.

The third reason to visit Trailside is that it borders on the Des Plaines River, and offers several walking trails alongside the water. You can take a peaceful walk—the trail is dotted with landmarks and signs, or find a comfortable place to sit and feel as though you're a million miles away from the city, instead of only nine.

This museum is perfect for toddlers and young kids who enjoy seeing relatively small animals—but it's also fun for older kids, especially those with a real interest in animals. They give free tours to groups of 10 or more, and teens who already work with animals in some capacity may be able to get a behind-the-scenes look at how these animals are cared for.

If you want to combine this trip with another point of interest, consider visiting the Trailside Museum on the last Saturday of the month, when Frank Lloyd Wright's Home and Studio—located just about 3 miles east of the Trailside Museum at 931 Chicago Avenue in neighboring Oak Park—offers its Junior Architecture Tours. These tours are for 6 to 12 year olds, and are led by specially trained 5th through 10th graders. Kids 8 and under must be accompanied by an adult. Tours last 45 minutes and cost $3 per person. Call 708-848-1976 for more information.

volo bog

❉ *28478 W. Brandenburg Road, Ingleside, IL 60041*

815-344-1294

Ideal Age Group: 4 to 18

Admission: Free

http://dnr.state.il/us/lands/Landmgt/PARKS/R2/VOLOBOG.HTM

a cool walk through ancient, soggy land

One of my very favorite places in the Chicago area is the Volo Bog State Natural Area—a National Natural Landmark—45 miles northwest of Chicago in Lake County. This relatively humble setting contains a world of nature and wildlife. Just off of Route 12—look for the Home Depot silo—this preserved bog—or wet spongy marshland with acidic water—holds everything from Canadian geese to poison plants (it's like a witches cauldron of murky water and plants). This bog was formed by a melting Wisconsin glacier and has been formed over thousands of years.

It's all free—and it's a great place to go and just hang out. You can sit on the docks of a small pond and get a close-up view of the life within. Or watch for the songbirds, waterfowl, and wading birds that stop by as they migrate north.

You can take a walk on the swinging one-half mile Volo Bog Interpretive Trail—which makes you feel as though you're an explorer starting out for the great unknown. This wooden path has small landing areas from which you can look over the expanse of the bog—or just pretend that you're on a pirate ship, crossing the muddy waters.

This trail takes you through all stages of the bog—you'll see moss, decomposing trees, tadpoles, poisonous plants, and bog buckbean and fern fiddlehead plants. Older kids and adults can make use of the Tamarack View Trail, a 2.75-mile path for hiking and cross-country skiing that traverses through woods, wetlands, field, and prairie. In spring and summer, you may see herons, cranes, whitetail deer, and mink—in addition to a host of flowering plants. In the winter, look for berry holly, deer, and red fox.

As an added bonus, the Illinois Department of Natural Resources hosts a visitor's center in a converted dairy barn on the bog grounds. Here, they offer education, exhibits, and hands-on learning to supplement what you'll see in the wild.

Try getting a printout of a list of the creatures and plants that hang out in the bog. Then see how many you can find. Or just keep your ears and eyes open. On a recent trip, we happened upon a turtle laying her eggs in the ground—and all the kids in the bog area gathered silently—and reverently—around. There are also small treasures to discover, like a butterfly garden, or small gathering in the woods to rest. You can pack lunches and eat at the picnic area (where pets are allowed).

If you've had enough pristine nature for the day, here's a strange juxtaposition—about a mile away from the Volo Bog and its natural beauty lies the Volo Auto Museum, a collection of antique, muscle, sports, and Hollywood film cars—including the Batmobile and KITT from *Knight Rider*. (They also have Michael Jordan's 1993 Corvette, with "23" on the side, and Marilyn Monroe's 1951 Pink Nash convertible.) So car and nature buffs can get two trips in here in Volo. The car museum is open every day and admission is $6.50 for adults, $3 for kids. (www.volocars.com; 815-385-3644.)

wrigley field

✤ *1060 W. Addison, Chicago, IL 60613-4397*

773-404-CUBS

Ideal Age Group: 5 and up

Admission: $12 to $36

www.cubs.mlb.com

baseball, life, and loyalty

When I moved with my family to Chicago as a child, I fell in love with the literature about Wrigley Field—how it was built in 1914 in the middle of a Chicago neighborhood; how the ballpark refused to get lights so as not to disturb those same neighbors (they gave in, famously, in 1988); and how the Cubs were America's lovable losers, embodying the importance of loyalty, persistence, and love of the game. Moving close to this magical place helped me to adjust to my new home.

My siblings and I made the trek to Wrigley Field from the suburbs several times a summer on public transportation—a big deal for non-city kids. After the metro train and a bus transfer we rode the Addison Street bus right to the entrance. Inside, we'd watch the game, eat a bag of sandwiches and Frosty Malts, and sing "Take Me Out to the Ballgame" during the seventh inning stretch. We'd always keep score, but it didn't really matter. The Cubs usually lost anyway. We'd get autographs and get sunburned, and share the game with other earnest fans—old men from the neighborhood scratching strikeouts and singles into their scorecards.

Today, you'll find much of the same. The famous outfield walls are still covered in ivy, the organist still plays, and the crowd still sings "Take Me Out to the Ballgame" during the seventh inning stretch. You can still buy hot dogs, and cokes, and keep score.

Of course, it's been updated too. The Tribune Company now owns the Cubs, and they added private boxes and upscale food to the menu. You'll also see many more fair-weather fans than the old neighborhood faithful. And certainly, it's more expensive. Game tickets range from $12 to $36 and parking is astronomical. But you can still get there by public transportation, and it's still the same old ancient structure, in the same neighborhood. (Perhaps you can never take the magic out of Wrigley Field—it was built on the grounds of an old seminary.)

It doesn't get much better than this for a kid in Chicago. Even though the lovable loser tag hangs by a string since the Cubs nearly made it all the way (and broke the city's collective heart in post-season 2003 play), Wrigley Field is still the great equalizer—we love the Cubs even when they lose, all the seats are good seats, and every fan feels that they could make a difference in a game (catching errant fly balls, or not).

It's also a place where kids can learn to slow down—and let life unfold. Baseball games still go as long—or short—as they need to. Pack your lunch, bring sunscreen and a sweater, and go with the right attitude. After all, you can learn a lot of patience and love from watching the Chicago Cubs play baseball.

Note: Avid Cubs fans should check out the behind-the-scenes tours of Wrigley Field—you can walk on the fabled fields and get a fly-on-the-wall perspective of Cubs' history. Tour stops include the clubhouses, press box, bleachers, and playing field.

*index

index

chicago's 50 best places to take children

index by neighborhood

About the Author

Clare La Plante is a Chicago-based writer, and co-author of *Heaven Help Us: The Worrier's Guide to the Patron Saints* and *Dear Saint Anne, Send Me a Man, and Other Time-Tested Prayers for Love*. She is also a regular contributor to *Chicago Magazine*.